Artists as Writers

Living and Sustaining a Creative Life

The Living and Sustaining a Creative Life series of books reveal the realities of today's artists and culture producers. These timely publications comprise essays that generously share innovative models of creative lives that have been sustained over many years. Their first-hand stories show the general public how contemporary artists, creative individuals and change-makers of the twenty first century add to creative economies through their out-of-the-box thinking, while also contributing to the well-being of others. Although there is a misconception that artists are invisible and hidden, the truth is that they furnish measurable and innovative outcomes at the front lines of education, the non-profit sector, and corporate environments. Intended to spark conversations across and beyond the arts, each path is an inspiring example that provides exceptional insight.

All of the contributors have been chosen by guest editors who are distinctive and generous in their own lives. It is my hope you enjoy each essay as much as I have. I believe they will surely inspire new avenues for artists to thrive for years to come.

– Sharon Louden, Living and Sustaining a Creative Life series editor

Artists as Writers
Living and Sustaining a Creative Life

Edited by Seph Rodney and Steven G Fullwood

Bristol, UK / Chicago, USA

First published in the UK in 2025 by
Intellect, The Mill, Parnall Road, Fishponds, Bristol, BS16 3JG, UK

First published in the USA in 2025 by
Intellect, The University of Chicago Press, 1427 E. 60th Street,
Chicago, IL 60637, USA

Copyright © 2025 Intellect Ltd

All rights reserved. No part of this publication may be reproduced, stored in a retrieval system, or transmitted, in any form or by any means, electronic, mechanical, photocopying, recording, or otherwise, without written permission.

No part of this book may be used or reproduced in any manner for the purpose of training artificial intelligence technologies or systems without written permission from the publisher.

A catalogue record for this book is available from
the British Library.

Copy editor: MPS Limited
Cover designer: Tanya Montefusco
Cover image: Erin Fostel, *Stairs (morning)*, 2021, charcoal and graphite on Rives BFK, 39 × 58 inches. Private collection.
Production manager: Sophia Munyengeterwa
Typesetter: MPS Limited

Paperback ISBN 978-1-83595-091-3
ePDF ISBN 978-1-83595-093-7
ePUB ISBN 978-1-83595-092-0

Part of the Living and Sustaining a Creative Life series
Print ISSN: 2516-3574 | Online ISSN: 2516-3582

To find out about all our publications, please visit our website. There you can subscribe to our e-newsletter, browse or download our current catalogue and buy any titles that are in print.

www.intellectbooks.com

CONTENTS

Introduction   1
Seph Rodney and Steven G Fullwood

Alexis De Veaux	7
Alicia McCalla	14
Angharad Coates	19
Ann Finkbeiner	25
Anna Mikaela Ekstrand	31
Bettina Judd	39
C. Travis Webb	43
Carla Whyte	49
Chiké Frankie Edozien	55
David Unger	63
Dylan Klempner	69
Elifete Paz	77
Glenn Adamson	83
Hakim Bishara	89
Hrag Vartanian	97
John Brady	107
JP Howard	116
Karen Taborn	124
Kathy Engel	130
Kealey Boyd	136
Khadija Goding	142
Kristine Rodriguez Kerr	149

Maaza Mengiste	155
Max S. Gordon	163
Odu Adamu	169
Ross Berger	176
Samiya Bashir	185
Samuel R. Delany	193
Seph Rodney	200
Steven G Fullwood	206
Sofia Maia Ciel	214
Travis Montez	225

INTRODUCTION

Seph Rodney and Steven G Fullwood

IF YOU PICKED up this book, then we're sure it's for you. If the last half century of self-help books flooding the market has told us anything, it is that people are interested in step-by-step instructions about how people become writers. Well, this isn't exactly that kind of book. It's better. Who needs a recipe when you can have rich stories from writers who *write* and accounts of what sustains them as writers?

Every budding writer wants to know about the journey to becoming a REAL writer, what decisions were made, which paths were taken, rejected, charted, and why. What magic keeps a writer writing? Maybe how many rejections did they receive from publications before that one life-affirming *yes*.

Follow, if you will, 32 stories about the circuitous roads that each individual took to earn the title "writer." Some you'll notice don't call themselves writers, yet. Telling someone you're a writer is often met with, "so, what have you written?" Many of the contributors in this book have wrestled with this and similar questions. What makes someone a writer and how do they sustain a living to make it happen?

The work of gathering a group of writers into this anthology who could answer this question began when Sharon Louden, editor for the Living and Sustaining a Creative Life series, reached out to us via email in 2019. It was her query that started the process: Would we like to solicit, organize, and write for an anthology that would continue the series, with a focus on writers? Now we only vaguely remember all the chats, meetings, invitations, follow-up messages, reminders, edits, revisions, and collegial arguments that make up the guts of this book. All of what is written here is a result of all of the above—which you will never see. This is very much the nature of professional writing, whether literary, analytical, poetic, expository, experimental, diaristic, or critical: The reader comes to it as a finished piece of craft. The reader doesn't see the discarded bits and pieces left on the workshop floor, the beveling of edges to make the joints true. There is a lot of sawdust we've swept away and machinery we've put back in their cubbies to present this varied and beautiful collection of stories. But here in our introduction we want to let you in on the nitty gritty of how we did it.

We created a formal invitation and started sending that out in the winter of 2019. In between that initial invitation and now, like much of the world, our call for submissions and writer deadlines were caught in the nettles of the "Great Pause": the COVID-19 pandemic. While the world set about trying to right itself through lockdowns, vaccines, and shutdowns, we too paused with the rest of the world. We had no choice.

But, in the middle of this, trying to find our way to fulfilling the mandate of this project we had phone calls, Zoom meetings, in-person lunches, and figured out how we wanted this anthology to look and feel. Rather than solely showcase the works of poets, fiction, and non-fiction writers, we deliberately solicited contributions from writers from lesser-known or explored categories in terms of writing genres.

When we got back on track, Seph, in his role as an editor at *Hyperallergic*, one of the key art publications in North America, used his access to reach out to curators, critics, and arts journalists. (Since then he has moved on from the publication to become an independent art critic and curator.) There are two of Seph's former colleagues from *Hyperallergic* included here. There is *Hyperallergic*'s editor-in-chief, **Hrag Vartanian**, an Armenian art and culture historian and writer, born in Syria, coming of age in Toronto and then settling in New York where he founded the magazine with his husband. And we feature *Hyperallergic*'s current senior editor, **Hakim Bishara**, a Palestinian expatriate who has had more and more varied jobs than most people we know. *Hyperallergic* also led us to freelance writers within the art scene such as **Kealey Boyd** who became a full-time arts writer based in Denver after almost a decade in the financial industry. And it led us

INTRODUCTION

to **Anna Mikaela Ekstrand**, a Swedish arts writer and part-time curator who founded her own online magazine *Cultbytes*, which she now operates as its editor-in-chief. Seph got connected to her by working with her on an essay published in *Hyperallergic*. **Sofia Ciel** also contributed to *Hyperallergic*. She is a Polish curator, lecturer, and writer who talks eloquently of the precarity of her educational and working life.

Also, embedded in the art scene is Seph's colleague **Glenn Adamson**, a former director of the Museum of Arts and Design, and an independent curator well known in the disciplines of design and craft, who met Seph at a gallery dinner in Chelsea several years ago. At a conversation at a Brooklyn art gallery in 2018, Seph met the younger writer **Elifete Paz** who writes about art and culture and how he sees himself navigating these shifting and demanding terrains.

Some writers featured here are adjacent to the art scene, including **Angharad Coates** who works in marketing, public relations, and institutional communications. **Dylan Klempner**, a former journalist and now a researcher into the clinical uses of art as therapy, talks about using art as a healing tool. **Ross Berger**, who has written plays, television drama, and short fiction, was linked to us through his partner who is a visual artist. Similarly, **David Unger**, who is a novelist, poet, and translator originally from Guatemala, also runs a program on publishing at CUNY in New York City and is married to a visual artist. He connected us to the novelist **Maaza Mengiste**, an Ethiopian-American who writes about the intersection of European colonialism and liberatory projects on the African continent.

Almost everyone Steven reached out to contribute to the collection he knew from his past life as a journalist, editor, and publisher. Most of those who answered his call were poets, activists, culture keepers, researchers, or academics. There are writers who thrive in the academy, such as professor-poet **Bettina Judd** and administrator-professor **Chiké Frankie Edozien**, and some comfortably outside of it such as multimedia poet, writer, collaborative artist, educator, and arts administrator **Samiya Bashir**, lawyer-poet **Travis Montez**, and the prolific journalist **Max S. Gordon**.

Some are wildflowers like journalist **Khadija Goding**, who created a zine while in her teens, filmmaker and activist **Odu Adamu**, and diarist-teacher **Carla Whyte** growing wherever possible, their spores able to ride the wind to their next gig as a filmmaker, performer, teacher, or freelance writer documenting their experiences for work, posterity, or their health. Many are polymaths.

The assortment of writers featured here was curated to stimulate possibilities for folks like you: individuals/writers about to take on the enormous responsibility of calling themselves a writer. "Write" is a verb, a truth revealed as you read how each writer in these pages forged a unique path to becoming a writer or a *person who writes*—and learns. The evidence is there in words of lawyer-turned-judge and poet **JP Howard** and Harlem historian **Karen Taborn**.

We wanted speechwriters such as **John Brady**, and science writers such as **Ann Finkbeiner**, and those who teach writing such as **Kristine Kerr**. We were gratified to have the work of **Samuel R. Delany**, an award-winning science fiction (sci-fi) writer with over 30 books to his name who is still writing. Among the most compelling accounts are those written by people who literally use writing to emotionally survive such as another sci-fi author **Alicia McCalla** who shares her heartbreaking story and the glimpses of light that sustain her through the written word.

Narratives of lifelong friends poet-writer **Alexis De Veaux** and poet-teacher **Kathy Engel**, both of whom have been writing for nearly half a century, appear in this collection, each offering supple and gorgeous renderings of their way with and *in* the word.

Because **C. Travis Webb** is such a careful and compelling speaker and thinker and someone who we've known for years through the podcast *The American Age*, we also invited him to contribute.

Because we sought distinct, unique voices, you will also find a range of racial identities, sexualities, professions, personal histories, and nationalities. Though many have settled in the United States, we have writers from Ethiopia, Guatemala, Nigeria, Palestine, Poland, and Sweden, as well as several who live all over the United States, California, Colorado, Georgia, Louisiana, Pennsylvania, Texas, and Washington. We weren't prescriptive about where writers hailed from, we just wanted to offer a platform to share the enchantment of learning how they found their way to lives they continue to want to lead.

As editors and readers, we were moved by the stories in this volume. One common thread linking each contribution is that these writers continue to write to meet deadlines, through grief, losing jobs, changing careers, breakups, moving, teaching, or simply the exigencies of making it to the next day. There are writers whose prose will immediately catch your eye and others that do not spark interest … yet.

We suggest that you give everyone a chance. Anthologies are designed so one can read it cover to cover, or here and there as the mood strikes. Again, this is not a prescriptive treatise, so we imagine that you will open the book to any entry and be engaged by the tools, strategies, and raw inspiration propelling each writer to share their poignant stories with us, with you.

* * *

ALEXIS DE VEAUX

FIGURE 1.1: Alexis De Veaux. Image by Steven G Fullwood.

LET ME SAY this:

I became a writer.
I grew up in a time in which I understood that being a black woman writer is possible. Then, as now, we have to be presented with the possible. Otherwise we cannot imagine, or reimagine, who we are.

I was 11 years old when I looked at Lorraine Hansberry, in 1959, the year her play, *A Raisin in the Sun*, was produced on Broadway. That moment constituted the first realization for me that black women *could* and *did* write. Before Hansberry, I did not know of a black woman writer. No miracle Phyllis Wheatley. No folklore voodoo Zora Neale Hurston. No Pulitzer-prize-winning Gwendolyn Brooks. Nobody. Because the literature of black *women* writers was not taught in my public school.

You have to *know* that something is possible in order *to become* the possible.

In 1960, I was 12 when I looked at my mother.
When I saw her trying to keep housed and clothed and fed a brood of children. A barely educated woman struggling with life. With little, often no, help from our fathers. When Harlem was called a ghetto. I looked at her one day I remember. I decided I would have a different life.

I taught my students to write by teaching them how to read.

This is how I arrived:
Growing up, I was always writing something. A story. A poem. A book report. I loved books—not just to read, but to have. I got a library card when my mother thought I was old enough to be responsible. I liked getting books from the library. I brought home armfuls of them. I didn't like having to return them though. I wanted to live with books.

By 1973, I was becoming the writer I wanted to be. That year, I published two books: a memoir, *Spirits in the Street* (Anchor Press and Doubleday) and my self-illustrated children's book, *Na-ni* (Harper and Row). I was 25 years old.

At that time, black writers were being courted by white publishers. We were the next lucrative market. They published us in droves. White publishing houses—at which a handful of black editors were employed across the industry—financially benefited from having an advantage over a hungry black readership. We were hungry for literature by black writers emerging out of the aesthetics of the Black Power and Black Arts movements. Movements which proved, over time, to be deeply nationalist, heteronormative, and misogynist.

I was supported by several othermothers. My paternal grandmother, Ruby Moore Hill, loved me unconditionally and taught me to read the Bible as poetry. Thelma P. Catalano gave me my first dictionary. Erna Sensiba, my teacher, loved me and risked everything doing so. The visual artists Valerie Maynard and Carole Byard gave me their eyes. The literary visionary Marie Brown. Mary Lou Williams sacred jazz musician. And there was Toni Morrison, without whose support … nothing.

In New York City, we were witnessing what became known as the second renaissance in black women's literature. The first had occurred in the neo-enslavement moment that was Reconstruction, which began in the 1880s and went through the early 1930s.

This is how I got *here*.
I remember reading the anthology, *The Black Woman* (1971), edited by Toni Cade Bambara. For me, *The Black Woman* became a formative counternarrative to the invisibility of black women's lives, histories, sexualities, and desires within the "black community." Bambara's anthology, her own work as a fiction writer, her activism on behalf of black folk, the fact that she was unabashedly centered in a community of other black women artists and activists—one she celebrated and was celebrated within—provided an early model for how to be a black woman writer:
Write your people. Their class as well as genders. Their poetics and their resistances.

There were shoulders I was standing on.
I never learned writing as a "how to."

This taking breath has meant I often encounter people who tell me they have read my work. Or that they passed a work of mine onto someone else to read. This journey has been life long and full of recognition, loneliness, honors, adventure, the sacred, the scary, and the mysterious. I have crossed generations and time. I am well known and not known at all. I am fortunate.

What I say to those coming after me:
You cannot seek the approval of others—your family, friends, colleagues, your peers, or your lovers. If you do, you will not write what you came to life to witness.

There are some things I will not write again.

I came into myself as a writer largely because of my mentor, the writer, Fred Hudson. Fred had come from the West Coast with a dream of nurturing black writers in a workshop setting. He created the Frank Silvera Writers Workshop, a key initiative of the Frederick Douglass Creative Arts Center, in Salem Church, on 129th Street in Harlem. The workshop attracted a number of eager, nascent, black voices. In welcoming me into the workshop, Fred daughtered me. We'd have long, cigarette-filled conversations over writing techniques, what books we were each reading, the city, Harlem, life, black politics. And by teaching me what he understood were essential tenets of writing ("show, don't tell"), Fred taught me to value my own imagination. To know who I was and what I wanted. That criticism was part of being alive. It made me stronger. There were times I thought Fred Hudson was queer. I was queer.

Be patient with your mentors.
Be more grateful.
One day you may outlive them.

This is what I have had to negotiate and bear and grind through:
Books are written one sentence at a time.

Expectations versus reality:
When I was new to this writing life, this taking breath, I would sit at my desk, with notebook and pen, and write for hours at a stretch. Writing is discipline. I taught myself to write by teaching myself discipline.
I lived on what little I freelanced. It did not fully support me.

Though I never believed in the trope of the poor and struggling artist, I believe I came to this life to be an artist. I have been homeless. Without food. Without money enough for the rent. Not sure if or how to go forward in this life.

Then I was in Cuba, in January 1985, as part of a delegation of black women writers: Toni Cade Bambara, Jayne Cortez, Verta Mae Grosvenor, Rosa Guy, Gloria Joseph, and Audre Lorde, among us. And one day, in between delegation activities, some of us were sunbathing on a hotel rooftop. And I expressed my doubts, the difficulties of this writing life, to Audre Lorde. And Audre said, "from what I've seen of your work you should keep writing."

This is what I have had to negotiate and bear and grind through:
Confidence is a body part.
You can grow a new limb.

I was 40 when I looked at myself.
I had a few teaching gigs here and there. But I was without the means to financially support my life. I had no health care. No savings and nothing to deposit. No social benefits of any kind.

I did not want to repeat Zora Neale Hurston: a black woman writer buried in an unmarked grave. I saw there were writers I knew who taught so that they could live the writing lives they wanted to live. I went back to school so that I could earn more teaching. In the fall of 1988, I entered the graduate program in the Department of American Studies, University at Buffalo, so I could save myself in the future.

There is some pain that writing creates.

Let me just say this:
Ask yourself: Do I want to be popular?
You have to have the stomach for isolation.

What the day to day looks like:

I have a room I go to and close the door. When I am in there, I have left planet Earth. To travel the cosmos. I do not write by computer. I write with a fountain pen in one of those black-and-white composition notebooks. Writing, like ink, is visceral. These days I go to my writing table when spirit calls me. When I am not at my table, I leave my room door open so that spirit can roam the house for inspiration. Or maybe just find a bite to eat.

Who mentored and mentors me:
All the black women, known and unknown, writing before me and after me. The shoulders I stand on.

I learned to feel for language, for the story that language tells.

What you taught me, Fred: the sound of what story feels. The sound of James Baldwin. Of Toni Morrison. Louise Meriwether. Henry Dumas. And Toni Cade Bambara who said, "People will try to trap you in a fiction."

I've always had a sense that writing was something I *had* to do. Like taking breath.

Write fiction. Write yourself into it. Like Octavia Butler, holy.

Forty years later, I still write because I feel like I have to.
I don't need to write in eight-hour blocks. At this point in time, I get too tired for all that. So, I nap.
Some days (or months) I write, some I don't.
When I am not writing, I am writing.
I am more interested in the erotics of writing now.
I write to pleasure myself.
When I am spent—whether by a group of words, a definition of a word, the ink on my fingers, the sentences or paragraphs I've been gifted on a given day—then I am satisfied.

The lives of your mentors are not fiction.

What this life produces in and through me another life did not:
It was the living you, June Jordan.
Who made me.
The aesthetics of your model of writing in and across multiple genres.
Who gave me the word "sovereign."
As the first step to understanding "abolitionist."

Who bought me groceries when I had no food.
And publicly encouraged me to take a leadership role in our Brooklyn community's politics. And wrote me notes about how much you loved me. And praised me as a writer. And said I was smart.

This is what has been produced in this life: the writer as possible. As black and feminist and queer and left-handed and sovereign and bookmaking the stories of our lives as black and queer and women. Evolving into and from the speculative future.
It is you in the afterlife, June Jordan.
Taking breath.

ALICIA MCCALLA

FIGURE 2.1: Alicia McCalla. Image by Dr Howard McCalla.

WHEN THE US NAVY showed up at my door on a Sunday evening on August 28, 2018, after my hubby and I had gone to bed, my world shifted. We were informed that our son had been lost at sea for many hours and that they were currently engaged in a search to find him. After several days, the search was called off and the Navy finally declared him dead. I was crushed.

This one event changed my life forever. Everything that I knew about who and what I was shifted. As a Detroiter and US Marine Veteran, I'd always believed I was strong … tough and could handle anything but my baby boy being lost at sea brought me not only to my knees but also my face and entire body flat on the ground, broken.

In grief recovery therapy, I learned when a loss occurs, it feels like a bomb has hit your residential home. It's ground zero. The place where your front door used to be has switched to an entirely different location. An incredible shift occurs. For me, it wasn't just a shift in my brain, but my heart was severed. Afterward, I experienced weeks of high anxiety, depression, and lethargy. A roller coaster of despair. Hard to come back from such sadness but I made the decision to try.

Anyone who knows me understands that I'm very organized and linear. As a school librarian, I found joy in maintaining the order within the library. But in my heightened state, I knew deep within my soul that I'd been changed for good and there was no way that I'd be able to return to my previous career. As much as I loved serving the students, teachers, and staff at my middle school, the anxiety attacks and depressive mood swings were a huge deterrent. So, when the discussion came up in grief recovery therapy, I emotionally unpacked and dug deep into what truly matters to me and that was writing. I decided to live a creative life.

For seven years, I'd worked full-time as a librarian and part-time as a science fiction and fantasy author. I'd published two novels and a series of short novellas. I very much understood what I needed to do as a part-time author but was very unclear of what I needed to do to make a living as full-time writer. I also had to deal with the elephant in the room. What to do about the shift in my brain as well as my gripping anxiety and depressive moods?

When my cousin stayed with me to help me get back on my feet, she'd create a daily checklist so I knew exactly what I needed to do. This daily list kept my anxiety in check. I had six to seven items to focus on and complete. Following the checklist kept me calm. When I decided to start writing full-time, I went back to that idea and a basic daily routine. I took my writing routine and laid it out in a manner that I could follow like a daily checklist.

My Miracle Daily Plan included the following:
(1) Before working I exercise (15–30 minutes) and meditate (1 hour).
(2) Record my start and finish times.
(3) Journal for 20 minutes (dump or purge all distractions and thoughts).
(4) Write gratitude statements (five or more).
(5) Be intentional and choose to perform one of the seven Sacred Gifts: Giving Away, Forgiving, Giving to Myself, Giving Thanks, Giving Forth, Giving Up, or Giving In.
(6) Read my Business Action Plan/Personal Goals.
(7) Create "to do list" (no more than seven items).
(8) Turn on my internal light.
(9) Complete the items on my checklist or go to work.
(10) Rate and evaluate my day.

Initially, my goal was to work five hours each day. I didn't want to overwhelm myself, but I needed a way to work intently without getting burned out. One technique that worked for me was the Pomodoro Technique, a time management method developed by Francesco Cirillo using a timer to break down work into intervals. I eventually settled on working for 45 minutes with a 15-minute break. I began with five Pomodoros per day but with this ritual, I'm now able to work an 8-hour day without feeling strain and anxiety. I'm also able to accomplish lots of tasks. My emphasis is on quality over quantity. I try not to push myself too hard because when I do, my anxiety attacks return. Instead, I take my time to set manageable daily, monthly, and quarterly goals. I break what I need to do down in the most bite-sized pieces so I don't have to struggle or strain myself. If I'm feeling overemotional or severe depression, I back off and relax my brain by taking a walk, reading a book, watching TV, or journaling. I don't make my days too difficult.

    My goal is to have fun and enjoy myself. I'd rather look up and think where my time went rather than struggle and strain throughout the day.

    Being overwhelmed is a big deal when living with grief brain. I make sure to keep myself very structured and organized when it comes to my general workflow. I religiously use iPad notes and Scrivener for writers. Both help to keep me organized and together. In my iPad notes, I keep a tally of what I've accomplished for the day (the headings or items are the same as on my quarterly business action plan), my daily "to do list" (from Miracle Daily Plan), and my Quarterly 90-Day Business Action Plan. I also use my iPad notes to easily copy/paste research notes, marketing plans or ideas, or anything that I need to maintain my writing business. Then, when I have a chance, I make notes or journal within my Scrivener files.

If you're serious about writing, Scrivener is magnificent. I have a Business Action Plan Project, a Current Work in Progress Project, and a Genre Research Project. I use Scrivener to write my novels, but I also use it to purge any and all ideas that aren't on my 90-day Business Action Plan to make sure that I don't wander off task. I have files for marketing, blog/website, new writing projects, and more. Anything that I find that fits within these categories, I drag and drop in these folders. Generally, I purge the ideas with a note or journal entry and when I'm ready to tackle that project, I have enough to develop a plan of action. This method has helped me stay focused and maintain a wealth of neat ideas for the time when I need them. I can't stress enough how important it is for me to maintain balance and focus. It's very easy to stray and get off task. This method of keeping track, purging all ideas, and putting them in the proper folder helps me stay very focused and most importantly, doing so keeps me calm.

During my days, I make sure that I take eating breaks. I generally eat two times per day and when I eat, I'm very intentional about the experience. I only eat organic fruits and veggies and grass-fed/grass-finished meats directly from the farm. Having high quality foods and supplements help keep me emotionally balanced. I can't stress enough how important it is to eat well when suffering from depression, grief, and anxiety.

Removing negative and toxic individuals from my life is extremely important when I'm so emotionally fragile. I learned quickly that it was best for me to cut down on my interactions on social media. I only use social media during allotted time windows then I shut it down and off. I unfollow anyone that has an overabundance of drama. I also cutoff or try not to answer any disruptive phone calls from family or friends, unless it's an emergency. Lessening these distractions keeps me focused and on-task as well as reduces my mental frustration.

I do need to make mention of setting daily, weekly, monthly, and quarterly goals. Every 90 days, I take the time to see what I've done for the quarter and think about what I'd like to accomplish for the upcoming quarter. I make my 90-day Business Action Plan. Then, I set aside time each month to check-in with myself to see what I've accomplished for the month toward those goals. I use the tally that I keep on my iPad notes to see what I've done, and I create a short report for myself so I can reflect. Every quarter, I send my report to my accountability partners and we discuss what I've accomplished and where I'm headed.

Accountability partners are very important to me. I continued working with my long-term accountability partner but I also added several writers who are full-time writers. I have an accountability partner with whom I speak with weekly on Zoom, and a face-to-face writer's group that I meet with weekly at Starbucks. This allows me to stay on track and communicate with others on a regular basis and gets me out of the house for an event other than grief recovery therapy or grocery shopping.

All-in-all, living with grief, anxiety, and depression is tough. Even more of a struggle is sustaining a writing life. For me, I've learned to create a daily ritual that supports my mental health and my creative life. Each one of these steps keeps me balanced, focused, and ready to live the life of a full-time writer.

ANGHARAD COATES

FIGURE 3.1: Angharad Coates. Image by Nolan Conway.

WHEN I WAS asked by one of the editors of this anthology to contribute an essay, I was surprised. Most people would not consider me a writer, even though I write all day long.

I am a communications strategist for art, design, and culture. I write press releases, pitches to media outlets, curator's statements, collection statements, crisis responses, copy for websites, bios, talking points for interviews—truly anything that will convey a message, even ghostwriting interview answers and drafting social media captions. My writing has to be succinct and immediately persuasive; I am trying to convince the reader that something or someone is important, beautiful, innovative, or just worthy of being noticed.

I'm not particularly precious about my writing. It's utilitarian, for conveying information as quickly and clearly as possible. Working in the art world, I came across so much incomprehensible prose that I became something of a clarity vigilante. I have read press releases for group exhibitions that failed to mention the number of artists in the show, curatorial statements that were obviously just someone's regurgitated master's thesis, and descriptions of sculptures that never used the word "sculpture." I can talk theory all day long, but it is too often deployed as a deliberately obfuscatory weapon. At one point, I printed out a tweet by the artist Wendy White and pinned it above my desk: *uhhhh if your press release says ur 'playing upon the transformation of visual information through layers of painting' that just means ur painting*. Kurt Vonnegut, one of my writing heroes, always said his own prose style was developed when he was working as a public relations man for General Electric. In his words (Shields 2011: 95), "A lot of critics think I'm stupid because my sentences are so simple and my method is so direct they think these are defects. No. The point is to write as much as you know as quickly as possible."

I would call my own writing style conversational, and I have happily sacrificed grammar for flair. Like most extremely online people, I'm not above using gifs, emojis, memes, hashtags, rap lyrics—truly anything that can convey meaning—to communicate. There are certain times that formal language must be used, but goddammit, writing should be fun to read. Once, in describing a major exhibition featuring a group of 1960s artists with an *épater-les-bourgeois* mentality, I wrote in the press release that there was "a fuck-you spirit to the whole enterprise," and cheerfully sent that release to critics at the *New York Times* and *The New Yorker*, to widespread amusement.

The most critical part of writing, for me, is not the actual pounding on a keyboard. It's being face to face with an artist, curator, inventor, or designer, looking at their output, asking them in real time about their personal history, influences, inspirations, and the adjectives they'd use to describe their work and then figuring out how to translate their ideas to a general audience. The question I am always trying to answer in my writing is, in the most mercenary sense, "Why should anyone care about this?"

There's a vogue now for PRs to describe themselves as storytellers, and like many clichés, it is in fact true. I am the person who gets to create the narrative around something and to shape the public's belief on a subject, with the thrill of going deep into research and teasing out the history and meaning of a project. To get to that moment of stepping back and asking myself,

> What is known about this, and what is not, and what should be known? What the hell is this actually and how am I supposed to present it to the wide world? What are the words I can use to describe it?

And then suddenly, in a flash, realizing I can tell that story through my writing? That dopamine hit can't be beat.

I have always known I could write; in high school in Boston I won writing prizes and while in college at Columbia I was selected for various writing seminars. Weirdly, however, I never had the dream of writing the great American novel or wanting to become a journalist myself. I am someone who didn't really have any real awareness of PR as a profession, and sort of stumbled into it after trying some other things, and then immediately discovered that I had a near savant level of competence at the game.

I started as a lowly assistant at a fashion house, and worked my way up to in-house head of comms at a major cultural institution, the New York Academy of Art, and later a managing partner for an international PR firm specializing in design. In-house writing, in which you are fully embodying the voice of the organization, is radically different from agency writing, where you are speaking on behalf of a client, and writing in different voices for a multitude of clients.

I've been ruminating on why I love doing specifically *this* kind of writing work, the pitches and the press releases. I think it's because I was always more interested in the signified than the signifier. I care not so much what something *is*, but what something *means*—historically, culturally, contextually, economically—how this thing directly influenced this other thing, what it portends for the future of these things, what the thing indicates about its creator's life or thought. For several years I worked in fashion (which is fantastic writing training, by the way), and I always said I loved it in both theory and practice. I was able to look at an Alexander McQueen collection, and realize "Oh, he's clearly alluding to Julia Margaret Cameron, and the concept of an idealized Britain, and there's a sly reference to New Wave and a witty nod to Yves Saint Laurent's bohemian moment … also, that's a cute fucking skirt."

People who work in PR are often dismissed as spin doctors, malicious gatekeepers, or slimy flacks who would sell their own mother for a story. Think of the Tony Curtis character in *Sweet Smell of Success*: a sweaty publicity agent wheeling and dealing to get his clients mentioned in the gossip columns. Are we histrionic anxiety bombs sucking down iced coffees while soothing a client and texting an editor that the fucking article went live with two fucking typos? Yes, assuredly we are. But we also care deeply about getting a story out there, and we sincerely believe that *this is cool and more people should know about it*. Ava DuVernay (Tingley 2019) has said repeatedly that her longtime career in PR was what made her successful when she moved into filmmaking, because she knew what stories weren't being told: "I spent 10 years learning how to amplify stories before I ever picked up a camera."

Some of my day-to-day work, other than the longform writing of press releases and statements, is a grind: sketching out the strategy for media campaigns, planning where I should go to offer the first exclusive and if they don't bite where to go next, timing out when to go wide on social media and websites, and thinking of all the potential angles to be activated around a particular project. When I'm doing this, I have to know which editors hate being sent PDFs, which ones get annoyed at being pitched stories about Old White Guys, which ones will get really excited about anything that has a local angle, which ones just had a baby so they can't cover anything that takes place at night, and which ones are inexplicably biased against any project involving a particular artist, possibly because that artist was rude to them once at a party. Sometimes an older or more experienced comms person would pass along this intel, but 99 percent of it you just have to learn by doing and getting to know the writers and editors and just ... being in the mix every day.

Like all professional writers, the other element that informs my writing is reading everything, all the time. I found pretty much the only profession that allows me to sit around and read magazines and newspapers all day, which is what I like to do anyway. I was indeed the 10-year-old weirdo who can be seen in a home movie reading *The Wall Street Journal* because I liked reading and it was there. It's important to be, for lack of a better word, a fangirl of writers: I can spew out to you my favorite recent pieces and have hard opinions on whose Substack is worthwhile and whose isn't. I recently loved Amanda Mull's (2023) exegesis on Bed Bath & Beyond's bankruptcy filing for *The Atlantic*, which had the immortal first line "On the first day of the rest of my life, I went to Bed Bath & Beyond."

Other than reading for love of the written word, I am also reading for a very specific purpose: to scent the way the wind is blowing. I read to see what's being covered, where it's being covered, by whom, what photos they're running with the article, what's a feature, and what's a small item. I read to see what publications are mostly just working with their own staff writers, and which outlets suddenly seem to be using a lot of freelancers these days. I read to see how certain trends are presented as news and others are not, or how a certain publication has mysteriously run five consecutive articles about the same thing. I have to be able to tell clients sometimes that no, that specific outlet will not care about a particular story, no matter how beautifully written the pitch or release is; they just won't.

As a part of this essay, the editors asked us to consider the question: "What will this life as a writer produce in and through you that another life could not?" There is always that sliding-doors moment of wondering what it would be like if I had chosen another life. But, very simply, this life allows me to just talk forever about the things that I love and am fascinated by. In a silly way, it is how I get my jollies—the absolute high of knowing that I'm sitting on a fantastic story and know exactly how to frame it. Most importantly, it allows me to be the vehicle through which the wider world learns about amazing projects and ideas. I cannot imagine another life.

Reference

Mull, Amanda, "You Will Miss Bed Bath & Beyond," *The Atlantic*, April 26, 2023, https://www.theatlantic.com/technology/archive/2023/04/bed-bath-beyond-closing-shop-replacement/673874/. Accessed June 17, 2024.

Shields, Charles J. (2011), *And So It Goes: Kurt Vonnegut, A Life*, New York: Henry Holt and Company.

Tingley, Anna, (2019), "Ava DuVernay on Moving From PR to Filmmaking, Directing 'When They See Us'", *Variety*, Aug 9, https://variety.com/2019/tv/features/ava-duvernay-when-they-see-us-2-1203295840/. Accessed September 18, 2024.

ANN FINKBEINER

FIGURE 4.1: Ann Finkbeiner. Image by Carl Finkbeiner.

IT HADN'T OCCURRED to me to be a science writer. I'd always been pretty sure I'd be a writer, but I thought maybe I'd write fiction or poetry, and so my education was in literature. I took only the science that was required—chemistry in high school and biology in college—and paid it as little attention as possible; I thought science was for people who didn't have the creativity to be novelists.

But like a lot of people who are pretty sure they're writers, I didn't see how to make money writing, nor did I know what I wanted to write about. So off I went to make a living, first to Detroit, then to rural central Pennsylvania, teaching English to junior high students in public schools, and later teaching in a program for gifted elementary and junior high students. I did this for over a decade and liked it well enough. I enjoyed watching students decide they liked to learn, but the job was exhausting.

In the midst of that, one day I was driving the Pennsylvania Turnpike from central Pennsylvania out to see my sister in Ohio. I noticed vaguely that in the Appalachians, when I was going up a mountain, the lines in the rocks exposed in the roadcuts also slanted up; and when I was going down, the roadcut lines slanted down. This seemed natural and I thought no more of it. But then in western Pennsylvania, out near Ohio, I hit the Alleghenies, and regardless of whether I was going up the mountains or down, the roadcut lines stayed flat. This did not seem natural and I, the literature major, thought "Why don't I know more about the world?"

This question seemed oddly urgent, and I thought I should act on it. So, because the schools I worked in encouraged teachers to continue their educations, I started taking night school courses: the origin and evolution of man, concepts of modern physics, principles of astronomy, the geological history of the earth. I saw clearly—I don't know why—that the evolution of hominids and the discovery of the uncertainty principle and the clustering of stars along the main sequence and the formation of the flat Allegheny roadcuts are all stories. They have plots driven by characters (though the characters aren't always people), and the tensions are between cause and effect, old ideas and new ones, theories and facts, and the one that became my favorite: the tension between technology, necessity, and morality. These stories were unexpected, nothing I could have ever invented myself, and they got me all excited. So, I signed up for a graduate science writing program during which I could write, be critiqued, then rewrite. Then I gave myself two years to freelance and make as much money as I'd made as a public school teacher. The money was pitifully small, and I still didn't quite make it, but never mind.

I did apply for jobs at magazines. As usual, the entry-level jobs were in writing news, which I tried to do and couldn't. Part of the reason was that I had no real background in science and am a slow study, so I couldn't write a story that was simultaneously accurate, substantive, organized, and met a short deadline. Another part was that I congenitally couldn't write news stories. I'm not sure why, but it isn't for lack of trying. Sometimes I have had to write them anyway and when they get edited all to hell and gone, not a word left standing, I tell myself I'm grateful to the editor and it's ok to have things I'm not good at.

Anyway, I found I could get assignments from magazines to write longer, feature stories about science under longer deadlines, so that's what I did. Between assignments, I got contracts to write for such science institutions as the National Science Foundation and the National Academy of Sciences. The writing was boring because the writer doesn't own the story, the institution does; but the science I needed to learn was interesting and has been useful. After maybe 10 years of alternating between features and hired-gun writing, I am now able to write only features. I mention this to show that age has its benefits, that hanging in there does work.

The obvious question: How can someone with a few night school science courses under her belt write about science? Wouldn't you need a degree in science? The answer is no. Much of what feature stories cover is new science not covered during a scientist's education, though knowing the basics ahead of time certainly helps, and understanding the culture would otherwise take years. But the sciences, especially the physical sciences, are logical. They're less an accumulation of facts than they are a history of observations and explanations whose sequence of steps makes sense. So, I take a long time, read a lot of background, try to recreate the scientific logic in my mind. I think until my brain gets exhausted, and I ask a LOT of questions. With time, the questions eventually get increasingly educated, but they start out in kindergarten. I tell the scientists I'm interviewing that my questions are elementary, but as it turns out, the scientists are surprised I have any questions at all and don't seem to mind answering them. (The scientists' attitude toward me reminds me of Samuel Johnson's quote about women preaching: "It is not done well, but you are surprised that it is done at all.")

When I feel stupid, and I always do, I remind myself of the times, years ago, when I'd sit next to an old physicist at a physics talk and ask him afterward how much of the talk he'd understood, and he'd say, "Almost none of it." I remind myself that physicists tell me routinely that they've rarely understood an idea the first time through, that they need to hear it over and over. I tell myself that the scientist is the scientist and I am the writer, and I wouldn't expect either party to know what the other knows. Besides, I don't write for scientists, only for ordinarily curious people.

I usually write about astronomy and cosmology but also about almost everything else, including: ecology, archeology, medicine, psychology, technology, geology, and the science of national security. The ideas for the "everything else" stories often come from the editors; I keep track of what's going on only in astronomy and cosmology. I read the general science magazines to watch how a field is evolving; I go to astronomy talks to hear specific research; I sit through days-long workshops to learn what the field thinks are the hot questions. In these cases, I know vaguely enough to propose ideas to editors. I've always thought that finding stories is extremely difficult.

For that and other reasons, I tend to write profiles of scientists. I always know which scientists are interesting people: They work on unexpectedly interesting questions; their research is understandable; they can explain it clearly; and they talk well. I want to know why they've spent their lives doing these difficult things, why they began doing them, why they keep on. If I ask these questions this way, their answers are usually mundane so I have to find sneakier ways of finding out, like asking how they happened to be working on a particular problem. I think of this process as finding their through lines. For instance, one astronomer said his advisor had told him to go off and think about the consequences of the universe being created in a hot big bang and cooling and expanding ever since, so he wrote a paper about that; but afterward, he said, he'd just jumped from one topic to the next. However, when I looked at his career, each new topic was the next logical consequence of a hot big bang. Finding these through lines is fun because scientists are often unaware of them.

For obvious reasons, I check the stories for accuracy *with* the scientists I interview. I don't say this too loudly or often or in crowded places because my journalist colleagues would put me on a rail and march me out of town. Journalistic practice is that sources of stories are never ever to be consulted after the story is written. But for me, accuracy overrules journalistic culture and I have no obligation to change any text I don't want to change. Magazines increasingly employ fact checkers though, so I now worry less about choosing between wrong details and outraged colleagues.

My day-to-day life is predictable, even boring, and I'm perfectly happy with that. I don't like excitement or unexpected interruptions. I travel when I have to but I don't like it; I don't even like going out to lunch. I need all my energy to overcome my limitations in brainpower and focus. I read and re-read, I list everything I don't understand, I interview scientists until I understand what I hadn't understood. I try to figure out the structure of the story I'll write; I never can until I actually write it. I write very, very slowly; writing is pure pain. I rewrite until I've memorized every sentence—happily I enjoy rewriting.

I don't feel I've ever been mentored. The person who would naturally have been a mentor was my graduate school advisor and we simply didn't hit it off. My view was that he needed me to be compliant and impressed and grateful, and none of those characteristics is conducive to being a writer—so I didn't have them and didn't want to grow them. His view could easily have been that I was a talentless bitch with an attitude. Either view works. In any case, I never expected to have a mentor, so I've never missed one.

This is not to say no one helped me. Every editor, with only a couple of exceptions, has been an enormous help. Every writer who accepted me as a colleague helped me convince myself that I am a writer. We do see ourselves the way other people see us, so everyone who has read what I've written and then responded has also been a help, so are all the people who casually say, "What are you working on?" These are normal social generosities, and I'm grateful for them.

My husband also supported me, both psychologically and financially through lean periods. He turned out to be a good reader of early drafts. He told me he was proud of me when I did well, and when I didn't do well, he'd encourage me. He'd tell me how excellent my job was, going out and talking to all these smart people about all these wonderful things.

And he was entirely right. My job is to find the people doing the most interesting work in the most interesting fields, ask them questions until I understand what they do and how it fits with the field's history and current state, and then write up what I understand. I think of this last step as arranging the little shrimps with tomatoes and lettuce until the platter looks irresistible. So, not only is the art and craft of writing stories, in the end, a delight but also the people I've met and interviewed and gotten to know are some of the most extraordinary one-offs that humanity has to offer.

The reasons my career went the direction it did, I still don't quite understand. The closest I can come is that the stories I can think up are never as inventive, meaningful, or pleasing as the ones that life and science come up with. I truly can't think of a way I'd rather live.

ANNA MIKAELA EKSTRAND

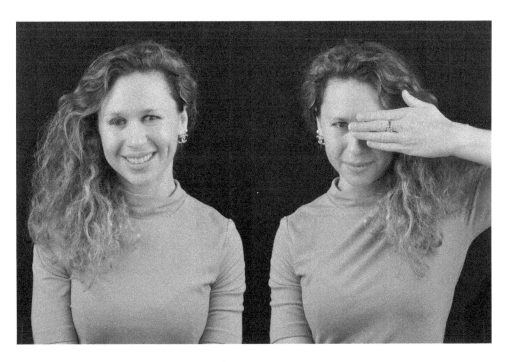

FIGURE 5.1: Anna Mikaela Ekstrand. Image by Dominique Duroseau.

OUT OF FRUSTRATION with the media industry's declining support of writers and a will to lead by example, I founded Cultbytes in 2014 as a platform where writers are paid and respected while being offered a space to grow and critique contemporary art. I was tired of dealing with stressed-out editors, pitching into what felt like the ether, tracking down small payments, and being asked for free labor for someone else's baby. I lost hope in changing publications through contributions so I birthed my own: an equitable art publication. In the beginning, the most common strategic advice I received was to have a specific focus—gender, media, region, racial, article type, whatever. It was half-hearted advice—*Interview* much? I did not want to arbitrarily curtail the kind of content I could feature based on what might be marketable. Being a multicultural, mixed-race feminist, multiplicity is in my nature. Surrounded by emerging artists, writers, and curators, I needed Cultbytes to reflect who we were by covering marginalized topics and responding to the times. I was thinking big and wanted to build my own inclusive community.

In the manner of so many other twenty-somethings trying to make it in New York's art world, I was always thinking ahead. If I founded my own publication, I would not need to rely on others to get published. I asked two friends to join the editorial board: Ayana Evans, a performance artist who was making big waves in the DIY performance space, and Alexandra Bregman, a Columbia School of Journalism student and reputable Asian art specialist who was also doing groundbreaking work on Russian oligarchs. I wanted to lift up their work and have them in my corner. That first year, I cycled through several names. Coming up with one that would last was *excruciating*. In August 2016, I was invited to cover *GLOBAL ACADEMY?*, a conference on alternative art schools organized by Summer Academy in Salzburg. The administrators and educators breaking conventions to create dynamic education systems that catered to the financial and emotional needs of their students and staff impressed a new sense of determination on me. Marking the end of several months of indecision, I noticed that the café at the local Künstlerhaus was called "Kult" and thought of *Cult*, a group of devotees, and *byte*—a unit of digital information. It felt right.

On the other hand, discussing editorial content with Ayana and Alexandra was a relief. "Write for me!" I told everyone

I met. Nina Blumberg, an early art influencer, who started the photography trend of people looking at art, was also a primary team member. I contracted her to manage Cultbytes' Instagram after she tagged me in one of her posts. The stakes were low and I worked with most, if not all, writers who showed interest. In those early days, I ran Cultbytes alongside my various other jobs and covered its expenses out of pocket.

I had founded Cultbytes to *set* standards not abide by them, so I implemented kind workflows. Most of my writers—including myself—were holding down multiple positions, so I adapted the editorial process to each individual, whether it be workshopping texts together or editing them, working with deadlines, or not, and accepting most pitches. I wanted to counterbalance burnout, unpaid internships, and not fall into the category of a project that lacked funding (which of course it was at the time), operating without compensation for work. So, I paid everyone. In the gig economy of artrepreneurs and multi-hyphenates, it is important to encourage work ethics that foster collaboration, support, and knowledge sharing so we who are not institutionally or corporately attached can share opportunities and advice in order to create our own free-floating collegial microcosms.

In the early 2010s before founding Cultbytes, I had written art criticism as a freelancer for some years—I pushed my way into art criticism, through the back door, or the press list, as it were. My first friend in New York, Christina, the daughter of a collector I had met in Paris, was a true Upper-East-Side-It-girl. Clad in her mother's vast wardrobe of vintage Versace, she was a young member of several museums and worked at Sotheby's. Holding only a museum job, I could not keep up with the high costs of the dinners, taxis, memberships, and benefits. I cut corners by getting tickets to benefits in exchange for posting about them on my Instagram feed.

At the Whitney Studio Party, in the fall of 2012, an art critic offered to introduce me to the owner of the online art publication *Art Observed* (AO). A few days later I found myself climbing the seven flights of stairs that led to *AO*'s office in SoHo. Michael, the founder—who bankrolled the enterprise through his real estate agency—greeted me and asked me to identify some of the artwork on the walls. A couple months prior, the art collector Adam Lindemann had pulled the same power move on me and when I misattributed a Richard Prince photograph to Wolfgang

Tillmans he went on the attack, questioning my competence to work in the art world. This time, I knew not to take the bait. I quickly scanned the room, recognized a couple of artists, listed them and proclaimed: "You have a mediocre collection of large edition prints. Let's start the interview." He hired me on the spot. I was learning how to hustle the hustlers.

Writing for *AO* led me to see writing as a craft instead of an innate skill. As I was paid $15 per article, I allowed myself four—then, when I got better—two hours to write each of them. From 2012 to 2014, I had to write faster than my self-doubt, not affording myself time to overthink things. I jotted down my ideas, copy-pasted segments from artist bios and press releases that I rewrote in my own words, and quickly moved paragraphs and sentences around to create cohesion. When I understood that I was spending too much time organizing and reorganizing, I devised two structural models for the different article types I wrote: reviews, art market news, and interviews. I created these formats by studying other well-written articles. While these texts were structured well, my language sometimes lacked finesse. In writing years, I was a toddler learning how to walk. I am thankful for our editor Daniel Creahan who helped me grow as a writer.

I experienced many firsts writing for *AO*: I conducted quirky interviews with blue-chip artists, carried out energetic live reports from Christie's and Sotheby's evening sales, and attended sponsored press trips. Beyond gaining access to things that I could not afford, contacting an artist or art professional on behalf of the publication offered me the opportunity to speak with them candidly. Writing allowed me to structure my chaotic life governed by the need to see *everything*—exhibitions, artist studios, parties, lecturing professors—which ameliorated some of the FOMO that marked my first years in New York.

While contributing to *AO*, I also had a full-time position as a research assistant for Susan, the founding director of Bard Graduate Center for whom I supplied research and writing support. Here I developed other writing skills—allowing the texts time to take shape as we uncovered new research—since our writing and editing processes extended over multiple years for some essays. Eventually, in 2014 and 2015, I moved on from *Art Observed* and Bard Graduate Center. For three months, I headed the Barnebys United States blog and wrote six articles a week on the clock to keep my payment-versus-time-spent-working ratio reasonable. I was in my element covering art, design, decorative arts, and material culture for sale at auctions. After my term, I was back to pitching and looking for work while continuing to run Cultbytes as a side project. Considering low or no writer's fees and staff writers being cut from publications in all industries, competition was intense and I soon realized that it would be impossible to survive as a freelance art critic.

In between jobs and in Cultbytes' early years, I had been balancing short-term marketing and public relations projects. I started off managing Instagram accounts, writing press releases, artist bios and statements, and placing articles. Two hundred job applications in, I realized that I was not going to find a position akin to the one I had at Bard Graduate Center and that I was in fact sustaining myself and my publication through public relations. I let go of my dream to work in a museum and embraced the dreams of my clients. To structure and make the work more transparent, I formed an agency. I created my own rules: I focus solely on digital media, work with art influencer marketing, and offer artists strategic career advice.

Now, I am seeing others catch up; more and more art critics publicize that they also work with public relations writing and many publicists abandon pushing print publications to focus on digital ones. I have yet to meet a freelance art critic who manages to publish the number of articles required to make a living wage. And many on-staff writers quietly, or overtly, bolster their wages with secondary income: advising, catalog writing, lecturing, and public relations. If you understand your field and can write, the bar to enter public relations is low. You can learn on the job. By this time, thanks to Nina, Cultbytes had a substantial following. When I expanded into public relations, a steady flow of clients were referred to me or slid into my DMs.

The art world is marked both by disillusionment—it is competitive and often poorly remunerated—and overzealousness. There is *a lot* of money on the move and a fair share of artists and professionals rise quickly. Feeding into these two contradictions and leading the way in utilizing multiple channels for his criticism, Jerry Saltz has been working unconventionally to engage audiences by participating in reality TV and documentaries, being active on Instagram, and frequently giving talks. His Pulitzer Prize helped him and his category (the art critic) gain celebrity both in the art and mainstream worlds. He is not the only one. Meme-artist Jerry

Gogosian's ironic critique of the art market has shaken the art world and engaged other audiences who want to get a glimpse of the more ridiculous elements of our industry. Taking a cue from Sarah Thornton's book *Seven Days in the Art World* (2008), Saltz and Gogosian's style of criticism alongside documentary films like *Exit Through the Gift Shop* (2010), *The Price of Everything* (2018), and *The Art of Making It* (2021) uncover the inner workings of the art market in a way that is accessible. Although it provides key insights, this genre often condenses multiple *art worlds* into the *blue-chip art market* overshadowing audiences, artists, and practitioners who operate outside of it. For instance, Grebnellaw, a Swedish performance artist is more interested in creating relationships between art, nightlife, and design through her practice than participating in the traditional art market. I bring these groups into focus in Cultbytes.

As galleries have fewer resources to support early stage artists, more rely on publicists to help them build their early careers. Since the art market is in overdrive and MFA graduates have increased, it is understandable that critics turn to public relations work to make ends meet. I find that many of my clients—mainly artists, galleries, and arts tech companies—understand the art market but need a media- and strategy-savvy consultant to get them to their next step. This makes responding to clients' needs in various team constellations both exciting and challenging. Press rarely drives up prices; rather it serves to engage audiences, legitimize, and, hopefully, bring context to the work. Often, more than placing articles, my work in public relations is about activating contacts and advising clients how to incorporate public relations into their day-to-day. It is essential for artists to have a digital footprint, and many tools make it easier to do public relations, not only social media platforms but also email clients, newsletter services, and advertorials. Creating debate around this shift in communications, some artists intentionally blur the boundaries between PR and art. Previously mentioned meme-artist Jerry Gogosian and Adam Himebauch's performance *Back to the Future* (2022)—where Himbauch created a fictive artist and promoted his retrospective through many posts on Instagram—incite necessary conversations around agency, gate-keeping, and truth.

I benefited from entering the media landscape during a time of change. During Cultbytes' lifespan, paid media has become legitimized, thus expanding revenue sources. Now, reputable journalists often work on advertorials and branded content. In addition, I have used social media platforms to bolster growth in our readership. Unfortunately, however, publications are struggling to find viable business models. Yet, they remain important, since we live in the information age. Communication is the most important tool in wielding power and building bridges, imperative in shaping our future. In addition, art and culture are bound to capital and wider socio-economic trends. As cities and states look to the arts to gain them international notoriety, attract visitors, and bolster their economy, the number of museums, biennials, and public art projects in the world has skyrocketed in the last 20 years. An increase in art-related university programs has trained many artists and art professionals eager to operate within existing and new frameworks that now, more than ever, crisscross the globe. As critics, it is our duty to uncover these geopolitical connections, pinpoint trends, and make sense of the many overlapping networks while highlighting artists and their practices. The industry's focus on the art market has created an environment that fosters favorable art criticism, subsumed by the PR machine. Instead of criticizing, many writers focus on topics that they can cover positively or neutrally. This is a disservice to criticism, the public, and artists overall that editors need to attend to with more fortitude.

Across industries, writers lately have been hit the hardest as they are taken off payroll and shifted to freelance. Social media marketing, especially influencer marketing, and advertorials have served to open the media landscape by allowing more artists and galleries to engage writers to critically consider and publicize their activities, on their own terms. Why pay for a one-page or a banner when you can pay for an article or an Instagram post with copy written by an art critic who engages the reader? In Cultbytes and many other publications, the advertorial is closer to a critical article than a press release or advertising text. Though the advertorial offers opportunities to make writing more financially viable, it also provokes ethical questions of objectivity, nepotism, and transparency to the surface—issues of much-needed discussion within arts media. The editor in chief of each respective publication is responsible for clarifying what content is paid for. Likewise, it is important to speak openly with art critics who work with public relations (there are many) about their modalities, ethics, and standards so that we take an active part in shaping a new responsible and sustainable landscape. Fostering relationships between art criticism and public relations is more challenging and important than glorifying one and trashing the other. To describe this new dynamism of public relations, criticism, and creative practice, adding to the many art world -isms, I ask you to consider PR-ism: public relations as a tool to navigate the art world, that will be part of the archive. This perspective opens up possibilities for increasing not only intentionality and experimentation in art, but also potential world-building, by allowing the accumulated material to become an extension of the artistic practice it supports.

That is a version of how I got *here*: in short, not staying in one lane and instead building opportunities. Whether by doing my part in shifting the dial of where digital arts media and its economy are moving, working with the next generation, or writing an interview, review, opinion piece, or book, I will continue to bear, merge, highlight, analyze, and distill art and culture in its various iterations while supporting new and old colleagues. I am also legally blind. I can see a lot, but I rely on others to help me when I cannot. But that is a whole other story.

BETTINA JUDD

FIGURE 7.1: Bettina Judd. Image by author.

WHEN I WAS in graduate school, I had a conversation with an elder mentor about the gift of mentorship. When I complained about the lack of available mentors for queer, Black writers, she told me, "Some people just don't get mentors—you have to mentor yourself." I was saddened and horrified. I was made aware of my apparent privilege as someone who never felt left without some kind of guidance. I was saddened because I knew there were folks out here with more skill and talent and promise in their writing careers, and they would just be out of luck— left behind because they lived in the wrong town, got caught up with the wrong crowd, or went to an uninviting school. I knew, I still know, how much mentorship means to me because I have a creative and scholarly career that touches on many fields—each of them with their own narrative and trouble with Black, queer women writers. But this is work I am called to do, and if I am not guided in one direction I must—I suppose—guide myself.

I am blessed. I have a coven, a hive, a siblinghood of friends who are as close as family who sustain me in this creative life. Beyond any singular workshop, residency, or academic program, these friendships (a few of which were forged in these spaces) have sustained me. But this is not just about the power of friendships— that seems well traversed enough—what is striking to me about these friendships and the way in which they have sustained me throughout my writing life is that they are *intergenerational, multidimensional, and free.* They are intergenerational in that I have writing mentors who are older and younger than me; of course, a number of them are in my age range as well. This diversity of age is made possible because the relationships themselves are multidimensional. Mentorship—as I imagine it here—is not a singular person who relates wisdom from a perch on all things related to my writing. No. I am not afforded that, nor would I wish to be at the whim of a singular supposed genius.

Instead, I am mentored in many different ways by different people for different reasons. This expansive concept of mentorship means that I do not rely on one overworked and beloved elder mentor to guide me through my creative career and minutiae of craft. It means that I allow myself to be open to the possibilities of learning from many people about what it means to write, produce art, perform, ask for money, file my taxes, organize my day, apply to that job, and so on. The fact that I do not rely on one person means that we are all free. No one is beholden to me, nor I to them beyond the politics of care that we share as people and most of all, friends and chosen family. In short, this view of mentorship—this free mentorship—could be better understood as a learning relationship.

To have an intergenerational group of mentors means that I cultivate relationships across age and experience in relation to my creative career and life. It also means opening up my perspective on what it means to have a career and life. So often I found myself career oriented and realized that anyone who has been a professional mentor of mine lives a life that I would not want to live. Bringing a balance to that means that I have to look to those who are living the kind of life that I align with. More recently, one of my dear friends who is a few years younger than me is traveling the globe—mostly through Africa, with a short stint in Europe. She started this journey just a year before the pandemic affected us all and has experienced the pandemic abroad. She is meeting new people, seeing beautiful sites, making professional connections as a worker in the arts, and generally living a lovely life. I couldn't imagine doing this myself, but talking to her helps me to imagine my life differently. It is not that she doesn't have responsibilities, she does. She made a choice, and though I may not know the kinds of decisions she made to do what she is doing, I can learn them from her.

In a similar fashion, I know of elders who are living their later lives in ways that I would like to see myself. Cultivating those relationships allows me to understand the decisions they made financially, personally, and socially. An intergenerational focus on learning from others allows for a vast network of people to learn from and people to share life with, which brings me to the issue of fostering multidimensional relationships.

To foster multidimensional relationships means to focus on the relationship aspect of learning from and with others. It means focusing on *the relationship itself as something to learn from*, as something which teaches me something about myself. Having these relationships also positions myself to teach, give, and serve in cooperative exchange. I can open up my friendships as moments of learning. I can open up my mentorships as moments of cultivating friends to care for, check in on, and be cared for. I appreciate this model since it is particularly powerful for those of us who exist in queer communities or have strained relationships with family, or simply have small families. The notion that we can only relate closely with and care for blood relatives serves institutions that would exploit us but does not serve the most vulnerable of us. My writing career has been largely supported by an array of mentors and friends, people for whom I would, in the words of Nikki Finney in regards to her mentor, Toni Cade Bambara, "hunt a tree down" (2003: 98). They have done the work to nurture me and in gratitude I am here to care for them in whatever way I can.

This multidimensional aspect of relating to others in mentorship also demands that I cultivate, within me, the capacity to be vulnerable to others, to admit when I do not know something, when I need help or guidance. I have to be attuned to my capacities for knowing and giving information as well as how to hush up and listen. Finally, this multidimensional aspect of relating to others demands that I share knowledge—that I do not hoard what I have learned, but that I allow the generosity of the circle that I have developed to spread to others. Multidimensional relationships necessitate such grace.

With grace comes a kind of freedom. Grace allows us to let go, to receive others freely and without demand. It carries with it a politics of care that would otherwise be reduced to transactional relationships. It allows us to be ethical in our engagement with others and ourselves. So when I say grace, I am gesturing toward a means of relating that is invested in freedom, which is not a freedom from responsibility, but a freedom to love and care for each other in circumstances what would otherwise disenfranchise us. It involves flexibility, honoring boundaries, and vulnerabilities. It involves an investment in the wellness of others *and* the self in resistance to forms of extracted labor that affect us all. It demands that we support each other.

To fully support each other mandates conditions in which we can all be free. It is a total concern, never compartmentalized because our writing demands it so. On a very basic and interpersonal level, it alleviates us individually from being harbingers of information waiting to be extracted. Relation resists extraction. We open ourselves to learning from mentees and mentors, giving mentors guidance and insight and bringing new mentees into our fold. With this kind of framework for mentorship and being a mentee, a friend, and part of a family, perhaps fewer of us may be left behind.

Reference

Finney, Nikki, (2003), "The Making of Paper," *The World Is Round*, Atlanta, GA: InnerLight Pub.

C. TRAVIS WEBB

FIGURE 8.1: C. Travis Webb. Image by author.

I sulked. Sulking is a big effort. So is not writing. I only realized that when I did start writing […] Not writing is probably the most exhausting profession I've ever encountered […] I mean if you're supposed to be writing.

—Fran Lebowitz, *Paris Review*, 1993

If you glossed it, jump back up for a second and spend a moment with what Fran Lebowitz said about writing in her 1993 interview with James Linville and George Plimpton.

I mean, there it is, right? Why you're here—Lebowitz's pregnant and inevitable qualification: "If you're supposed to be writing."

You've picked up this book about living and sustaining a creative life through writing, so presumably you've already decided you're *supposed to be* writing. Sympatico! I supposedly feel the same way.

Still, it's worth thinking about for a moment.

There are a lot of other things you could be doing. Going for a walk. Reading. Watching a movie. Masturbating. Curating your social media. Painting your masterpiece. Studying for the LSAT. Getting and spending. Trading up. Trading in. Trading off. Loving your neighbor as yourself. Or much better, yet, researching the perfect pair of inserts for the boots you're going to wear on that dream trek across the Camino de Santiago.

You know the trip, don't you? The one where that super-duper, self-actualized version of yourself absolutely, fucking radiates sexual potency, cultural omniscience, and spiritual equanimity in the Spanish sun.

Come on, you know that trip. We all have that trip.

But you're not doing any of that. You're here, with me, reading about writing. So, let's be real about it for a couple thousand words. What are you really doing here?

Seriously. What are you doing here? You're going to die—like, soon. I know you know that, but do you *know* it?

In fact, from a certain point of view, say that of general relativity, you're already dead, and so am I. We just happen to be in the same inertial frame so it looks to us like we're both alive. Although, depending on when you find this book, I might not be.

But let's just imagine for a moment we are alive to one another. You and I—all of us—even at the apex of our powers are always already on our way to that somewhere else we'll never actually be. We don't know how many trips around the sun it'll take to get there, but the destination is inexorable. Like eggs in an ovary, the number of days you have in that carton of years you call a lifetime was set long before you were old enough to read or understand that what you're reading might not literally be about the thing you think you're reading about at all.

So, look, when you pick up a book about creating and sustaining a creative life through writing the first thing you need to come to terms with is the "life" part. Keep at least one eye on the possibility that there are other things you could be doing with it.

The "creative" part kind of takes care of itself. Look around you. The whole damned world is an artifice. It's all "creative." It's not just the museums, the writing workshops, the poetry readings, or the Banksy-ed apartment buildings. If you think for one second that the Verizon customer service rep you just argued with for 20 minutes isn't a bonafide Picasso in some aspect of his, her, hir life you're probably an asshole.

Is he, she, xe a transcendental genius? Probably not. But neither are you (probably), so let's just call it even. Any primate who can successfully make the transition from a toothless, diaper-wearing, milk siphon to an adult who believes that Donald Trump can MAGA, or that AOC is so woke she can turn the Rust Belt Green, deserves our admiration for their creativity.

Our respective capacities to shamelessly summon fantasy before the merciless banshees of history is one of the few canonical miracles I can get behind. And although it does occasionally commit a genocide, circumcise a 12-year-old girl, and turn melanin into a metaphysical proposition on value, I'd say on balance I'm a fan of our boundless creativity.

That covers the living and the creating, so let's get to the writing. What does it mean to be a "writer"? I consider myself an expert on this subject because I've spent the bulk of my adult life not doing it, so I can personally attest to Lebowitz's observation that it is mentally and spiritually exhausting to avoid it. The way, I would imagine, being homeless is exhausting.

As a writer, I confess a sense of entitlement to the bounty of human achievement, and regretfully but unreluctantly claim my own awful portion of the persecution, suffering, and injustice that shapes our collective history.

If I can extend my sympathies to the fifteenth-century Harrapan shepherd who stood in terror on the Gangetic floodplain as horse-riding marauders descended on his farm and he wondered if his wife and daughter would be raped and murdered or only raped while he and his sons lay dying in the mud, then I will claim a cultural kinship with Harriet Tubman without apology even as I acknowledge that some not-so-distant "23andMe" cousin was a member of the Klan in Arkansas and let his weird little Euro-American pecker rub up against the negress his family saved up to own until he convinced himself she wanted to be raped.

The world is gruesome and delightful, even if the proportions are askew, and I'll stretch my sentences as far as they'll go to spelunk for the shiny bits. I'd encourage the same for you.

In return, I promise to use my little lies to tell the biggest truths I can manage. I hope you'll do the same.

We've got to look out for one another. It's easy for our self-conscious gyrations to lead us astray when we've been yoked with the feeling that we're supposed to be writing. It is, as Lebowitz said, exhausting when we refuse its call. But it can also be exhausting when we heed the call only to become overly preoccupied with other people's pursuit of the same calling.

Let's be honest, though. We're talking about a certain kind of writing, aren't we? You wouldn't be reading this essay if you were just wondering how to slam out an app review for *Wired*. Not that there's anything wrong with that kind of writing. That's most of what humans read, and I appreciate an elegant turn of phrase about the evolution of skeuomorphic design in mobile apps as much as I appreciate it in a Samuel Johnson essay about character. Dexterity with words is to be admired where it's found. But we're talking about something else. We're talking about how to *live* as a *writer*, which is presumably very different from living as a fireman or an engineer, which should also not be confused with *making a living* from writing.

So here it is. Here's my advice for becoming the kind of writer who writes because they feel exhausted when they don't. You need to build two homes. One home is not enough for the kind of writing we're talking about. You'll need two.

One for living. And one for dying.

And this home here, this writing-home that you're so drawn to, is your dying-home. The further this home is built from your living-home, the more space you'll have for it and the less space you'll need for the other.

No offense to your living-home. We all belong to *some* nation, *some* class, *some* ethnicity, *some* profession, *some* culture, *some* gender. Even if you reject these things, embrace your universal humanity or pan-sexuality, *some*one else will assign them for you. You might not like it, but that's the game. Get ready to duke it out, start a revolution, burn a flag, or dress in drag. Everyone is ready to kick Descartes around until it comes time to admit they're not autonomous minds reasoning their way into their own freely chosen identity—then they're all for Cartesian dualism. You're the pro-socialsty of the prosocial primates, so other primates get a say in who and what you are. As the cliché goes, they brought you into this world, so they're happy to take you out.

Like I said, you can fight over your identity, if you want to—and, honestly, maybe you should. *Some* of us really are standing in the way of what you want. And it's not always ignorance, or education, or fear. *Some* people just don't like you. Or maybe they do like you, so they want you to dress like they do. Or maybe they really, really like you and don't want you to burn in hell. I probably wouldn't want you to burn in hell either if I went in for such things. Maybe I'll join you in fighting these people because as fate would have it, my thinking evolved like yours and it's the neighborly thing to do, but don't believe your own progressive propaganda. It's gonna be a war.

But in your dying-home, there is no war, just you surrounded by nobodies and no ones out in the vast emptiness that is everyone's native land—a place that has never been colonized by any idea or liberated from any oppressor. The more time you spend here, the more garish your living-home becomes. With all its social coordinates, performances, and manners, when you return to your living-home it will sometimes feel oppressive, humorless, and rigid. But because your dying-place is empty and limned with words, you can really open up and love your guts out.

I mean, my god, there's just so much space out here! You can even bring some of it back. It won't be missed by anyone. I promise. Try it. A scintilla of that nothing is like a metric ton of love. Even the largest vanities vanish inside of its unconditional event horizon.

Unfortunately, a lot of people who write build their houses too close together, and their living gets all tangled up and grown over. They become heavily invested in the sum of their social relations. This happens especially when writers are paid to write. It doesn't have to happen, of course, so if you get paid well enough to cover your rent by doing *this* kind of writing, propitiate whichever cosmic entity will secure its future and keep right on doing what you need to do—but remember to revisit your dying as often as possible. Consider putting some daylight between your two homes to remind yourself that you share kinship with every other thing that is, was, or will be. Even your ancient cousin, the rock, was there once and will join you there again.

Or, if I might make one last suggestion, if you accidentally built your homes too close together, go ahead and tear down the dying-place you've got going and start over further out there.

It might take you forever to find the perfect nowhere, but you've got forever for this place.

Time isn't the same out here. Forever is a nothing.

Don't worry—you can leave your living alone. It'll take care of itself. Just go along with some crowd and keep things from getting too out of hand.

But when you're alone, seek out your cabin in the dark, just you and your emptiness trekking into the night's wild indifference with all the courage that you can muster and all the words that you can carry.

You might get lost, lose some things along the way, or this place might swallow you up whole. But if you're lucky it will break you open, make a stranger of your mother, turn all your convictions to dust, and leave you scattered across the hills.

CARLA WHYTE

FIGURE 9.1: Carla Whyte. Image by Avery Werther.

I WRITE BECAUSE, for such a long time, in many ways, I have felt like I couldn't speak. To me, it makes perfect sense that I'd direct a good friend of mine to a blog post I'd written to deepen his understanding of what I was trying to say, rather than just tell him what I was trying to say as we were on the phone.

"Please read it," I told him.

"I'm more vulnerable when I write than when I speak."

I was venting to him about my frustrations related to dating: It's day 3207 of quarantine (at least it feels like it) and a dead-end conversation with some guy put me in a moment where it felt like the universe was a DJ holding down a wild party on a Friday night, where the crowd is totally cutting up, and he is screaming into his microphone, "You still single!"

Single like a dollar bill. Even during quarantine, when many people are not working and probably have the most unprecedented amount of free time on their hands as a collective, in a hyper-capitalistic nation, I still can't get a text back.

Those were my thoughts at that moment, not considering that this is a rough time for a tremendous amount of people who, yes, may have more free time, but might also have to now contemplate how they'll pay their rent, how they'll feed children, how to regularly share a space with an abuser, how they'll bury a loved one …

Per usual, my friend brings me back to reality and reminds me "it's not you, it's them" and I mostly believe him because, as I told him earlier, I've come a long way from where I was last year when I would often internalize every disappointment as a reflection of my own self-worth. Only within the last year have I been able to make a slow climb from what felt like very deep, dark pits of insecurity, feelings of worthlessness, negative self-talk, and self-deprecating thoughts. Still, I wanted him to read my blog post … I feared being completely raw and vulnerable over the phone because … it's hard?

Four hours later, John emailed me a one-pager with paragraphs of targeted thoughts and feedback demonstrating that not only were my thoughts and feelings very clear, but that he could also relate to so many of them. Initially, I was elated knowing that I had shared some of the deepest, ugliest parts of my inner thoughts and that the reaction was positive. When I told John how happy I was that my feelings were relatable, he didn't hesitate to tell me not to prioritize relatability over realness.

"Fuck relating to other people. Be your authentic self and be honest. Would it be nice to be relatable? Yes. But don't think that your experiences, thoughts, and feelings are not valid if people don't relate to them. They're yours."

Read me, John. Read. Me.

So many things I'd heard from family and schoolmates contributed to my tendency to "tone police" myself: You talk like a White girl; you think you're smarter than everyone; you're evil; you're ungrateful …

At home, dissent was equated to betrayal and disrespect. At school, my speech was likened to Whiteness and "goodie-two-shoe" behavior. Subsequently, I didn't feel like I could be vulnerable anywhere, but I did want to belong somewhere, so at home, I wrote my feelings in my journal. At school, I dimmed my light to not draw attention to the parts of me that weren't acceptable. I created short stories about a young girl loosely based on my life and who I wished to be. Her name was Fatima. She had a chocolate-brown complexion and was an honor roll student who lived in a nice house in Brooklyn with her father and younger brother who she protected faithfully. She helped others, her boyfriend Raheem found her irresistible, and her father was so proud of how mature, responsible, and kind she was. Fatima's presence was golden to her father.

If I had to choose, I would have to say that my childhood desires to belong, to be loved, and to be accepted are what brought me to this very moment. They brought me here. My inability to confidently speak up and be bold with my mouth is what made me impeccable with my pen.

For almost a decade, I've worked as an educator in several countries in Africa, Asia, and Europe, and in a few charter schools in New York City. My desire to share my experiences with Black and Brown children in the classroom stemmed from the discomfort I felt as a young adult in numerous professional spaces where I was often one of few or the only person of color. I believe that representation matters and that it could be impactful for urban Black and Brown children to learn about things like international travel, study abroad, the Peace Corps, etc. from someone who looks and/or sounds like them. That was my bottom line, which I quickly lost sight of once the school year was under way back in 2015, the first year that I taught at an NYC charter school. Prior to 2015, schools that I taught in abroad did not demand as much of me, with regard to lesson plan expectations, behavior management, and responsibilities outside of my primary role, which was teaching. Prior to 2015, I wasn't required to monitor children going up and down steps on my break. I wasn't required to facilitate a small literacy group. I wasn't required to supervise lunch. I wasn't required to attend weekly coaching meetings. I wasn't required to supervise recess. I shared nothing with any school leaders except my lesson plans. I was just expected to teach my classes and the rest of my time was mine. Charter school was a different beast.

At my first charter school, I was learning new historical content, internalizing at least ten different nonfiction texts weekly. I was a graduate student. I was now having to learn and uphold punitive behavior management systems that felt problematic and excessive. I was working extremely hard to serve children and impress school leaders, so it was frustrating when I felt like I wasn't doing either one adequately. These emotions have persisted throughout the last five years, and I did reach a breaking point which manifested in my abrupt resignation from a charter high school where I was the 10th grade global history teacher and the grade level leader. I had so many ideas and dreams for myself and my students, but it was hard to keep sight of them when I struggled to deliver on the primary outputs of my role as a teacher. So, I left.

By no means am I proud of having abruptly resigned from my role in the middle of the school year. Everyone knows that it's frowned upon, and I certainly had many conversations with myself in moments of utter exhaustion where I tried to cheer myself into pushing through to June. If I had to identify the reason it became impossible to push through though, I would have to say that somewhere along the way the demands of being a teacher in "high-performing" charter schools overtook me. I lost sight of my bottom line in trying to be successful by the standards of this institution and subsequently my investment dwindled until I ultimately folded. The last few weeks away from the classroom allowed me to clear my head, reflect, meditate, rest, write, and reacquaint myself with my purpose for being an educator. It also allowed me to rediscover my passion for telling stories with my pen, stories about real life and stories about what I believe life should be.

My daily life looks very different now: it consists of waking up and going to sleep at unconventional hours. Sometimes I'm bored. Sometimes I feel extremely inspired. I've been journaling a lot more and through journaling, I've been able to be more in touch with my thoughts, feelings, desires, and goals. What has become abundantly clear to me is that at heart, I am an educator and there are certain aspects of my teacher life that I do miss … like preparing engaging lessons about history for my kids and having discussions about the parallels between life in the past and life in the present. The sociologist in me nerds out about rich lessons like the one where I have students simulate the scramble for Africa as I prime them for studying European imperialism and colonization. Simultaneously, the sociologist in me wants to share stories about the ways in which charter schools often miss the mark in their pursuit of "liberating" children from marginalized backgrounds.

While a part of me enjoys educating kids, another part of me also endeavors to share and curate stories: through Instagram, through a blog, through a podcast, through speaking engagements and workshops …

I don't just see myself as a classroom educator. I see myself as a storyteller. My obligation is to share important stories, and, in some ways, I have been doing just that in my classrooms over the years: I've shared my stories of what it's like to move through spaces as a minority Black woman so that my kids could understand that experience and possibly seek guidance when they find themselves in those same spaces. I've shared stories about being a single, unmarried, Black-American woman to my students abroad who thoroughly believed that I was at risk of dying in America every day. I've shared my stories about international travel on four different continents with students and friends who have never left the country and think that every trip abroad (outside of the Caribbean) probably ends like the 1999 film *Brokedown Palace*. I've been sharing stories and simply hadn't realized, until now, that much of my inspiration for my stories comes from my travels and from the adolescent classroom. Now, it seems like my mission ought to be figuring out how to regularly curate these stories and get them to different audiences. Stories are for sure worth being shared. I believe that doing so would allow me to feel like I am completely walking in my purpose. I don't believe in hoarding one's knowledge and experiences because self-knowledge is meant to be shared.

In a sense, this very moment is probably the beginning of my trajectory as a teacher-writer-influencer. Ha! No, but seriously—up until this point, I have sustained myself monetarily as a teacher. And because I see my students as the source of much of my content, I do believe that I will find my way back into the classroom for a time. However, now that I have a clearer vision of my purpose as a storyteller, my task has become prioritizing the creation of a space where I actively and deliberately curate those stories. It's no one else's responsibility to do so but mine. My stories are what I will leave on this Earth for posterity. I simply can't allow myself to have so many thoughts and ideas and keep them to myself. As I mentioned before, to be stingy with my knowledge is unfair if my life's purpose is to share.

It's both exciting and scary to think about the additional responsibility that I'm now charging myself with because back when I was a teenager, imagining my life as a 30-year-old writer, none of the things that are actually true of my present life were a part of my teenage dream: I'm unemployed at the moment; I don't know what the "next thing" is that I am going to do, nor am I "successful" by societal standards, or the standards of teenaged Carla. However, I'm doing the work. This is the part that absolutely no manual was written for. No degree could have prepared me for the introspective work that almost all of us will experience at some point in our lives where we must take a long, deep look at where we are, unlearn much of what we thought we knew, and realign with our spirit to figure out where we want to be. My only hope at this point is that I continue to obtain clarity and sustain my vision as I forge onward: Share stories. Share Black stories. Loudly. Boldly.

CHIKÉ FRANKIE EDOZIEN

FIGURE 10.1: Chiké Frankie Edozien. Image by New York University.

— *Lagos, Nigeria, sometime around the second World Black and African Festival of Arts and Culture.*

There once was a popular soap opera called *The Village Headmaster*.

It aired weekly on television sets all over Nigeria in the late 1970s. It made millions howl with laughter. It was appointment viewing in those heady days just before and after FESTAC '77, before Nigerian movies made in Nollywood exploded and sucked up all the onscreen entertainment in Africa.

I quite recall sitting on the floor to watch a small black-and-white television in our living room at 27 Lugard Avenue, in Ikoyi. Back then Ikoyi was mostly residential. And bucolic. And, compared to now, it seemed sparse. There was little traffic on its narrow streets and the large trees provided shade to pedestrians.

A lot of families who lived there were civil servants, and our home was just steps away from the Public Works Department. A sprinkling of expatriate families, diplomats and the like, with cars that had red license plates, also lived in the area. But their kids went to even more posh private schools than Home Science Association School.

At breaktime, all the pupils of Home Science on Ruxton Road would spill out into the courtyard and dish. It was all about what we saw on television the night before.
"Did you see so and so do such and such on *Village Headmaster* last night?"
"Ehn hen. Did you see when Amebo said."
"Chai!"

The character of "Amebo," ably played by Ibidun Allison, was at once harmless and corrosive. A purveyor of information, an embellisher of truth, she oozed innocence and insouciance. She was simply the village character who sold you palm wine and dropped gist to go with it. A town crier wailing information most wanted to keep private. She couldn't help herself; she always had to share. And share. And share.

Or at least that's how my pre-teen mind saw her. And till tomorrow many Nigerians of my generation, and the one before, will derisively brandish those who they feel can't keep their traps shut as "Amebo."

I was fascinated with the drama playing out each week on screen. Just as I grew more and more drawn to the drama in the pages of the newspapers that my father brought home from work most weekdays. When my brothers were playing soccer on the field in the compound, I, the youngest one, an asthmatic, buried my face in newspapers.

—*Port Harcourt, Nigeria, sometime between 1981–86 and 1986–89.*

Well, boarding school at age 11 is not the freedom from tyranny my little head imagined. Everyone is my senior. Everyone can punish me. It seems everyone does punish me.

Older boys gobble my provisions before the next Visiting Day. For that matter, I may not even get my mother or any visitor the next Visiting Day. I have to fetch buckets of water to bathe and the toilets, well, they are holes in the ground. They are just the pits. To use them I have to squat. And dodge accidents.

At dawn it's morning jogging, then bathing, then breakfast, then class, then lunch, then siesta, then afternoon prep (study time), then dinner, then night prep, then lights out. Rinse and repeat, weekday in and weekday out.

Get me out of here!
But then, two years in, something changes. I'm no longer in the most junior class. This peculiar federal government college (high schools are called colleges here and, in this era, boarding schools are tony) feels like home away from home. I've bonded with some classmates and unbeknownst to me I am making lifelong friendships. I've blossomed and I'm blossoming into a sometimes smiley, sometimes surly teen with opinions.

I have things to share about the big wide world out there—after all, I've been on holiday twice to London for "summer."

And at least two rich kids bumped into me and my family as we shopped at Brent Cross Shopping Centre, so I'm now cool. I want to tell stories. But I'm no "Amebo." My stories will be different. They will help me and my fellow students get things from the principal and his team of tyrannical teachers. They will inform us. So just like the stories from the newspapers, I begin to write and present stories for the Press Club at the school assembly.

Am I gossiping when I talk about a teacher who recently got married and changed her name, or about the septic tank that has never really worked and which school authorities ignore?

No! I'm just doing my work as a press person!

Since I'm no good at sports and have not much to do with the interhouse sports or school sports outings, I can go as a press club member and write something for the bulletin. I'm now a senior and several regional boarding schools have been grouped for competition.

Calabar.
Abuloma.
Ikot Ekpene.
Port Harcourt.
Owerri.

There is no way I'm going to miss the regional CAIPO games as a participant. It's a badge of honor. And since I live for the drama, I signed up for the drama club. I shine on the stage.
No. Actually I dazzle. I come home a winner. And then high school is over, and those pesky exams get in the way but, somehow, I end up at the University of Port Harcourt dancing and prancing my way on stage at "The Crab" theater. I'm in the theatre arts degree program. I'm acting at school and auditioning back home in Lagos. I'm actually getting bit parts on nighttime shows. I'm an actor. I'm a writer. I am 19 years old. I am broke.

Nigeria is bleak. Economic troubles. Military dictatorships. Everyone who can check out checks out. I have no plans to, but when I go on a long-promised holiday to America, I don't bother going back. Broadway beckons. I am an actor. I am a writer. After all.

—Syracuse, New York, USA, sometime in the 1990s.

Being broke in Syracuse is humiliating.
"You have an accent."
"Where are you from?"
"You are African aren't you?"

I put down my Broadway dreams and I do well in school. I'll never get any roles on stage with this accent. But I'll write well. I hope. It's cold. It's horrible being a janitor. It's better being a phone operator: "AT&T, may I help you?"

It's mindless work but I can do it at night and go to class in the daytime. I go see Afrobeat mega-star Fela Anikulapo-Kuti in concert at a New York City venue and the Syracuse chapter is over. I pack my bags soon after.

—New York, New York, the 2000s till …

The city was so great they had to name it twice. It is full of possibilities. And has pockets of blackness in all its brilliant glory.

I'm home.

It has pockets of gay people in all their brilliant, rainbow glory.

I'm home.

"Come closer," the tall, bespectacled one with the long cassock says loudly, arms outstretched. This man is a Catholic priest speaking from the altar of his gorgeous gargantuan Jesuit parish in Manhattan.

He's asking the gay men and women to move right up to the front as this house, that is God's house, is theirs too. I'm home.

I am a writer. Not an actor anymore. But I'm a journalist, recounting and retelling stories for newspaper articles. I make a living. I battle with editors who I believe have an "anti-" agenda. I wonder whether their sole *raison d'etre* is to demonize people like me in print.

But at this tabloid, with a circulation close to 700,000 readers daily and a very influential readership, I see firsthand the power of having my stories published. I write about us. I write about them. I write about the powerful and the downtrodden. I battle with editors who never seem to understand us.

In down times, of which there are many, books save me. I face my demons by taking responsibility and delving into more books. I enjoy *A Return to Love* by Marianne Williamson and swear by it even though my friends think she's kooky.

Years pass.

I amass a body of work. I'm proud of the changes I've made through my journalism. I am a writer. And now, I'm a teacher too. I understand that context matters in all stories, and I try to get my students to never forget that.

—Accra, Ghana, 2008, then sometime in 2014, or maybe even 2015.

Traveling through Africa, I see that state-sponsored homophobia is all the rage in some countries. I see that religious zealotry is driving policymakers and influencers blind. If only they knew. I am a writer. So I write more magazine articles—more journalism.

It's not enough. It seems to have little impact.

"Kill the journalist. Write about you."

That's the counsel from my dear "broda," Binyavanga Wainaina— advice he wails at me in New York too when he's visiting the Big Apple and we are having a nice dinner at CookShop, a bustling restaurant in Manhattan's Chelsea that is full of beautiful people. All of them are skinny.

All of them are dressed like they are off to a fashion magazine photoshoot. We sip wine and take it all in.

He is a writer, a memoirist, a storyteller. He's celebrated. And he's talented, yes, but he's also just brilliant. When he visits me in Ghana and tells me about his essays and new book as he makes fun of my fuzzy relationships, he says some version of "write about you."

When you write about you, you can give context, it seems. You can have an opinion. So I look inward. Maybe I'm interesting enough to have a story worth sharing?

I write about growing up and falling in love with a man in Lagos who doesn't have the courage to buck the system, so he gets married to some girl. The work is published in an anthology, *Safe House: Explorations in Creative Nonfiction*, edited by Ellah Wakatama, OBE.

Ellah's a unicorn.

Ellah sees me.

She gets my stories. She needs little explanation or justification. Ellah calls me on my shit. And it's all done without a scintilla of humiliation. She doesn't buy my varnished, rosy picture of getting de-flowered at sixteen by an eighteen-year buddy who's now a preacher man. Her notes as she edits allow my writing to be truth.

Ellah is a magnificent unicorn.

Or perhaps I've never had a good editor until now? Perhaps I'm only just becoming a writer now? Years later, she edits a different project based on fear. The light touch is still there. Well, the touch: heavy when it needs to be and light when it needs to be. It's a joy and I'm constantly learning not just about craft, but about life. How did it come to be that in trying to do my best work I found a unicorn walking among us? I don't block the blessing but embrace it.

The lessons help me with other pieces and other editors, like the incomparable Sunila Galappatti.

And then when John R. Gordon, who edited my memoir, came into my world with his meticulous and insightful thoughts and ideas, I am already used to looking deeper, digging deeper, and am open to ways to get my copy even more sparkling in its honesty.

—*The Bronx, New York, autumn 2019.*

I am a writer.

Imperfect yes, but striving and capable of soaring higher than I'd ever imagined, and all the while nurtured by a family of contemporary African writers-cum-journalists and editors whose general excellence I glean from: Chris Abani, Jennifer Nansubuga Makumbi, Maaza Mengiste, Zukiswa Wanner, Diriye Osman, Kinna Likimani, Nii Ayikwei Parkes, Sulaiman Addonia, Sisonke Msimang, Abubakar Adam Ibrahim, and Leye Adenle, to name a few. If you don't know them, don't gloss over their names. Find their work and bask in their literary glory. Do it as a favor to me but, really, you'd simply be treating yourself.

—*Tamale, Ghana, winter 2019.*

I am a writer.

I'll continue to shine a light on stories some choose to ignore. With the thousands of visitors flocking to Ghana to mark the 400th anniversary since enslaved Africans arrived in America from these coasts, many of the stories have been about the horrors of the dungeons and the slave ships. The world had never seen anything like it. The majority of these visitors don't stray far from the coastal areas. But I write about places the captives were taken from, places the slave traders never visited, close to the Sahara. Hundreds of miles away. I show how far their tentacles turned communities against each other and the living scars of places whose residents never saw the sea before they were taken there.

I tell the story of a horror trail often ignored. I give them their due.

I am a writer.

An acting life may or may not have afforded me this joy. I have some ways to go.

I hope to become a better memoirist too.

DAVID UNGER

FIGURE 11.1: David Unger. Image by Maj Lindstrom.

MY PARENTS DECIDED to emigrate to the United States in 1955, shortly after a CIA-engineered coup ousted Jacobo Árbenz, Guatemala's democratically elected president. Our departure had all the trappings of a flight for political reasons, but the truth was much simpler. With all the violence and terror, real and imagined (there was a lot of disinformation), it was impossible to run a business that asked people to risk their lives to have dinner out. My parents had three young children and La Casita, the restaurant they operated for years, went bust.

I was four years old when we arrived in Miami, not speaking a word of English. The paradise that I had inhabited in Guatemala—full of mountains and volcanoes, *frijoles negros*, bicycle riding in front of the National Palace, zoo visits—disappeared. Along with my brothers and parents, I had to negotiate a world that was foreign, aggressive, and racialized. So many fights initiated because someone—often a southern cracker—called me a spic or a dirty Jew.

Coming to the United States was seismic—disorienting and traumatic enough to make me a kind of double agent who silently observed life as I lived it. I became a keen spectator who mostly guarded his observations, sometimes even from my parents and brothers—they had an equally tough time adjusting, but they didn't develop the writing skills to describe their alienation.

I survived grade school and high school in Miami, thanks to summers spent in Guatemala in the late 1950s and early 1960s living with my grandparents. My brothers and I relished the freedom of walking the safe downtown streets of a modern capital. We lived in a kind of cocoon—almost owning the streets—before Guatemala devolved into a 36-year armed conflict from 1960 to 1996 in which 200,000 mostly Indigenous people were killed or disappeared.

* * *

In high school, I gobbled up an unorthodox medley of writers, including A.E. Houseman, Lao Tzu, Dylan Thomas, and John Steinbeck. I dabbled in writing poetry in college and by the time I entered Columbia's MFA program in creative writing in 1973, I was a serious silk-scarf, whiskey-breath poet. Outside of class and work, I read Rimbaud, Baudelaire, Dickenson, Michaux, Plath, Hikmet, and dozens of Latin American poets. I co-translated and edited two books for New Directions press by the time I was 35. But as translation is an underpaid profession, I survived by teaching GED math in a Bronx drug rehabilitation program and poetry in public school classrooms for Teachers & Writers Collaborative. Then in 1980, I began a three-year stint teaching English at the Walden School.

My poetry manuscript "Neither Caterpillar, Nor Butterfly" had been a first finalist for the 1978 Walt Whitman Award, offering publication and a $5000 prize. Judge Louis Simpson promised to get it published for me, but then reneged. Luckily, I was well aware of the great and noble Latin American tradition of self-publishing your first book of verse. Unlike Chileans Pablo Neruda (born Neftalí Ricardo Reyes Basoalto) and Gabriela Mistral (born Lucila Godoy y Alcayaga), however, I didn't appropriate a Hispanicized pseudonym like Roberto Márquez, which surely would have gotten my 1985 publication more attention in the Anglo world.

Discouraged, I gave up on poetry. Translation kept my writing chops sharp and allowed me to bring into English works in Spanish that deserved a wider readership. Over the years, I've translated 18 books, mostly written by women (Guatemalan Rigoberta Menchú; Mexicans Silvia Molina, Elena Garro, and Bárbara Jacobs; Cuban Teresa Cárdenas; and Brazilian Ana María Machado, to name a few). In 2022, my retranslation of Guatemalan Nobelist Miguel Ángel Asturias's "Mr. President" received glowing reviews in *Harper's* and *The Washington Post* and went into a second printing within the month.

In 1985, I co-founded the Latin American Book Fair, which, through four successful editions, brought dozens of Latin American writers and thousands of titles from Nicaragua, Cuba, Mexico, and Argentina to New York. Those were heady days—hundreds of Chileans, Argentines, Colombians, and Uruguayans forced to leave their homelands lived here. On 14th Street alone, there were three important Spanish-language bookstores: *Las Americas*, *Macondo*, and *Lectorum*.

When the book fairs lost financing in 1994, the Guadalajara International Book Fair (FIL) hired me to beef up its international reputation among publishers, writers, librarians, booksellers, literary agents. My tenure with the FIL coincided with its growth into the most important Spanish language book fair in the world, one with a huge international presence. I have enjoyed my sales work because I am selling a product I wholeheartedly believe in—Latin American books and writers—and my job doesn't conflict with my own writing as editing books might do.

In 1998, I became the director of the Publishing Certificate Program (PCP) at the City College of New York, a program whose mission is to increase diversity in the publishing industry. With the support of CCNY alum Walter Mosley and then CCNY President Yolanda Moses, we were able to get many publishers including Penguin Random House, Hachette Book Group, and W.W. Norton to support our program. Up until now, the PCP has graduated 450 students, half of which have worked at least a year in publishing. Most of our graduates are from diverse backgrounds: African American, Latino, Asian, and most recently South Asian, African, and Eastern European. The PCP has undoubtedly made a marked impact in increasing diversity in the publishing industry.

* * *

All this is a long way of saying that I never had the time or the luxury to write fulltime. I stole hours from my jobs and, also, would get up 5:30 in the morning when I knew where my writing was going. I won't say that my five novels came easily to me, but once I knew what I wanted to say, I wrote quite rapidly. Early success has spoiled many a writer, but I published my first novel at the age of 52. In 2014, when I was 64, I was awarded Guatemala's Miguel Angel Asturias Prize in Literature for lifetime achievement, this though I don't live in Guatemala or write in Spanish. The conferring of this award truly fulfilled many of my dreams to reconnect with the land of my birth.

I am not at all bitter or angry about my path, nor do I feel resentful that I haven't had more time for writing. I write when I have something to say, and I don't know what I would do if I had the luxury of being a full-time writer, feeling the pressure of a contract or writing simply to be published. Because I write almost exclusively about Guatemala, my readership is mostly in Latin America and Europe. Brooklyn's Akashic Books has published two of my novels in this country, but more than anything, I labor here in anonymity.

William Blake wrote in his 1793 edition of "The Marriage of Heaven and Hell" that *One law for the lion & ox is oppression.* I think that each writer finds an accommodation between the muse and the demands of the marketplace and family (I have two daughters, a stepdaughter, and five grandchildren). I understand that a writer like Tillie Olsen resented motherhood and domesticity because after fulfilling her parenting obligations, she was too tired to write. I get that. Nevertheless, this has not been my experience. Fatherhood and now grandfatherhood were not imposed upon me forcefully and so they have been, and are, a source of great pleasure.

I get all the nourishment I need from novelists and poets, some of whom I translated and others simply read: Melville, Vallejo, Rilke, Austen, Lao Tzu, Roque Dalton, Agustín Lara, Gioconda Belli, Nazim Hikmet, and Delia Prado.

When I was at Columbia University back then, I generally wrote poetry in opposition to my mentors, some of whom were considered illustrious poets. I got more out of reading and drinking with New York School poet Frank Lima and translating and drinking with translator Hardie St. Martin, than I did studying poetry with David Ignatow, Stanley Kunitz, and Maxine Kumin. I think of mentoring as what I got out of my reading, always keeping in mind, T.S. Eliot's (1919) dictum "Immature poets imitate; mature poets steal; bad poets deface what they take, and good poets make it into something better, or at least something different."

It's important to not only recognize one's accomplishments but also be grateful to the people who helped along the way. My parents, Luis and Fortuna, gave me strong family values and the guts to engage and struggle. Writer and editor friends like Paul Pines, Denise Phe-Funchal, Raul Figueroa Sarti, and Salar Abdoh were always there to support me. I don't think anything came easy to me—I matured late, in a rather unorthodox way, but I don't resent my decisions. I am as happy washing dishes as I am writing and translating.

Going forward, I hope to translate a few more books before I hang up my hat. I may have another novel in me. One about Jacobo Árbenz and the 1954 coup that changed my life.

For every door that shut, another one—better, wider, and more welcoming—opened. It's important to acknowledge that.

I am reminded of Frank O'Hara's delicious 1950s poem "Autobiographia Literaria":

When I was a child
I played by myself in a

*corner of the schoolyard
all alone.*

*I hated dolls and I
hated games, animals were
not friendly and birds
flew away.*

*If anyone was looking
for me I hid behind a
tree and cried out "I am
an orphan."*

*And here I am, the
center of all beauty!
writing these poems!
Imagine!*

References

Eliot, T. S. (1919), "Philip Massinger," *Times Literary Supplement*, May 27, Part I.

O'Hara, Frank ([1950] n.d.), "Autobiographia Literaria," https://allpoetry.com/Autobiographia-Literaria. Accessed April 25, 2024.

DYLAN KLEMPNER

FIGURE 12.1: Dylan Klempner. Image by Charlotte Kesl.

FOR MORE THAN a decade I have explored the intersection of the arts, medicine, science, and culture, as a journalist, a scholar, and interdisciplinary artist. In my role as hospital writer/artist-in-residence, I provide creative activities at the bedside for adult patients, caregivers, and medical staff. Most of the patients I meet with endure lengthy hospital stays that separate them from their homes, jobs, families, and friends. I offer them and their caregivers opportunities to share stories or focus their attention on personal art projects instead of on their pain and discomfort. Now based in the Washington, DC area, I continue working in the fields of arts and health with Medstar Georgetown Hospital's Arts and Humanities program. I also frequently teach creativity workshops with community organizations such as senior centers. Since the start of the pandemic, much of my healthcare-based work has been facilitating creative workshops online.

How I chose to become a writer and artist who works to inspire others to be creative begins with my own loss. My mother, Lynn Fontaine Klempner, died when I was 3 years old. As a result, I have been keenly aware from the moment I first came into consciousness that life presents unanswerable questions with which we all must cope. Losing a parent at that age oriented my perspective toward making sense of the past. The way she died—she took her life—also meant I needed to make meaning of and grapple with difficult realities. Artistic expression was a central part of my childhood. My father, David Klempner, is a musician and there are writers, poets, glassblowers, and many painters on my mother's side of my family. Writing, particularly, has been the best method for processing and understanding facts, while attending to and making peace with life's mysteries. At the same time, the arts have provided opportunities to build relationships with loved ones, friends, and mentors.

I learned early in life that the arts offer opportunities for self-expression and comfort in times of stress. My father, who began taking drum lessons at age 7, played professionally in bands until I reached school age. Raised in a conservative Jewish home, my father converted to Evangelical Christianity prior to marrying my stepmother, Rowena Klempner, when I was 5 years old. My dad often played drums for the worship services at First Pentecostal Church (which later became Christian Life Center) in Springfield, MA. Once, he was asked to sit in on drums at another church during a revival with a visiting evangelist. At one point between songs, the musical director turned to my father and asked him to imagine his drums were filled with the devil. The thunderous sounds from his drum solo reverberated throughout the sanctuary. I was filled with pride watching him play because he seemed to embody a particular passion and skill that was distinct to him.

I was also exposed to the arts through my grandparents and extended family. Many of my earliest and happiest memories include spending time with both sets of grandparents. My father and I often relied on their support after my mother died. As a single father to a toddler, my father moved us in with his parents, Harry and Rosalyn Klempner. My maternal grandparents, Marie and Raymond Fontaine, and I also remained close. Starting when I was 4 years old, they invited me to visit them a couple times each year.

My maternal grandparents' home on Cape Cod, MA was filled with family members' artwork. As far back as I can remember, I wanted to be able to paint like my great-uncles, Bill Maloney (my grandmother's brother) and Joe Fontaine (my grandfather's brother), whose impressionist landscapes of Boston and Cape Cod covered my grandparents' walls. My grandparents often took me to my great-uncle Bill's gallery shows, where he would sometimes put on painting demonstrations. During an art opening in Chatham, a few people wandered around the small garden that surrounded him. Some stopped to chat and laughed as he joked with them. I focused on the brush in Bill's hand and on the evolving image on paper: a soft, colorful depiction of the white bench and blooming lilac tree in the near distance. I thought of him as a kind of magician. By putting paint to paper, his connections with the landscape seemed deeper than ours, his life a little richer.

Having no idea how artists develop, I became obsessed with finding my own hidden talent that I hoped God, or some teacher, might reveal to me. I took music lessons, in guitar, piano, and drums. A few times, I sat down with pencil and paper to draw, but I didn't know where to begin. My drawings looked nothing like my uncles' artwork, so I put the drawing materials away. I never asked my great uncles or cousins for help or guidance. I was too embarrassed. I thought I simply lacked any talent.

In addition to being a drummer, my father is a writer. He and my stepmother moved my half-brother John and half-sister, Rachel to Jacksonville, Florida in 1987, when I was 14. For many years, he worked as an assistant minister to immigrant families at a large Southern Baptist church there. In the late 1990s, he self-published an autobiographical book about his conversion. Throughout my teenage years, I watched him work on the book, his draft pages spread out across the living room floor.

Writing was something I did from an early age, first, at school, for practical reasons (to do well on my homework) and later for more expressive ones. I spent a lot of my school age years with a desire to please God so that he would find favor with me and guide my life amidst confusion.

I never understood why my beloved grandparents—Jews on my father's side and Catholics on my mother's—weren't eligible for heaven in the eyes of the evangelical church. Eventually, my doubt and discomfort, especially about this issue, caused my faith to crumble into agnosticism. But during high school, writing was an important part of my spiritual life. I went to Christian school and was an active part of my church's youth group. In school, I wrote poems about God for English class assignments. I also sometimes filled devotional notebooks provided by the church's youth ministry with my thoughts about sermons and Bible passages, hoping to uncover God's plan for my life.

During my senior year at Babson College, I took a creative writing class with poet Mary Pinard in the fall of 1994 that proved to be a turning point in my creative life. I wrote for myself. For the first time, I lost myself in homework, staying up late to finish short stories or to fill notebooks with handwritten copies of poems by writers I admired. I developed a journal writing habit then that I continue to this day. Writing my thoughts down in a journal helps me reflect. When in my early 30s, I went through a divorce, writing in my journal about the ways I felt I had been injured and about my shortcomings as a partner—along with psychotherapy—helped me process my grief.

During undergraduate college, I also observed how my aunt, Patricia Fontaine turned to the arts to experience its healing qualities. Her example had an enormous influence on my life and work. Patricia was first diagnosed with breast cancer in the 1990s and subsequently dealt with multiple cancers over several years. One Thanksgiving, while she was undergoing chemotherapy treatments, it scared me to see her wearing fleece hats over her shaved head. Yet, throughout her recovery process, Patricia often relied on creative practices. "The ability to create a story with word and color makes something come clean and clear from grief and stress," she once wrote to me in an email.

"They become the ingredients for a story that we then get to sort and name, rather than the story telling us how to think and feel." After she had recuperated, Patricia began teaching art and writing workshops for people dealing with cancer and other illnesses at Hope Lodge in Burlington Vermont and at Central Vermont Medical Center, in Berlin, Vermont. Years later, I would follow Patricia's example, teaching writing and art making workshops in healthcare settings, particularly for those affected by cancer.

In 2005, I enrolled in Goddard College's MFA in interdisciplinary arts program hoping to find my voice as a writer and as an artist. At Goddard, I was encouraged to explore ideas and to allow the mediums I used to arise out of larger meanings and intentions. I was encouraged to experiment with new media and to run up against the limits of my comfort zone. The faculty were often my role models, particularly painter Peter Hocking, who writes novels, and poet Gale Jackson, who paints. Working with new media had always been mystifying and scary. At age 30, the first time I painted with oils at Peter's studio in Providence, RI, my hands shook. My ego put intense pressure on me. I was still looking for some latent talent to emerge and terrified that it wouldn't, not understanding that my early failings as an artist were simply due to a lack of training and practice. In time, Goddard's faculty helped me refocus my fear of failure by helping me consider the social implications of my work. That training began to bear fruit after a series of losses persuaded me to shift the focus of my creative work away from myself.

In 2007, the death of my last grandparent, my maternal grandfather, Raymond Fontaine, coincided with the breakup of my first marriage. I stood beside my then wife in a courtroom three days prior to losing my grandfather. For several months afterward, I tried to process my losses and rebuild my life. In time, I had a desire to use whatever skills I had developed to serve my community. I chose to pursue journalism by taking online classes at the University of Massachusetts. I interned, then freelanced, at a local newspaper, the *Daily Hampshire Gazette* in Northampton. I felt as if the stories I told for the paper gave me a clear role in the community while putting my own experiences into perspective. As a reporter, I wrote dozens of articles about all sorts of people and events. I announced the opening of new businesses, covered local elections, and profiled artists, farmers, and injured soldiers returning from Afghanistan.

While living in Amherst, MA I spent many nights during the years 2004–09 attending the writing teacher Pat Schneider's workshops, which were often held in her living room. Schneider founded Amherst Writers and Artists (AWA), a nonprofit arts organization whose mission is to support established and emerging writers (especially those who have been silenced or marginalized) through the use of a method for writing and teaching that she describes in her book, *Writing Alone and with Others*. "Every person is a writer, and every writer deserves a safe environment in which to experiment, learn, and develop craft," Schneider writes. Pat's workshop method encourages participants to write together for several minutes and to immediately read aloud what they put on the page. Because the work is new, participants respond only with positive feedback, focusing on what they like and remember. To protect each person's privacy, their writing is also considered fiction unless they say otherwise.

Pat's method is not about creating a perfect piece of writing in the workshop. Instead, it helps establish and shape communities of writers by providing a safe space for them to freely share. The positive, instructive feedback teaches writers new skills without criticism and builds writers' confidence to return to old work and continually start again. In my own experience, the method doesn't get rid of a writer's inner critic but empowers an encouraging voice alongside it. When I offer writing activities for hospital patients and caregivers, I use Schneider's approach. Encouraging creativity and our shared human experiences by focusing on process and personal expression matters more in healthcare and community-based settings than polishing finished pieces.

While working on an article at the newspaper, I interviewed artists, Rick Lowe and Wendy Ewald. Lowe was in Amherst to co-teach a course on community-based art practices with Ewald. Having grown up in family of artists, I was familiar with how art can facilitate joy, distraction, and meaning. But Lowe and Ewald's work suggested that art could also be used to address people's practical needs. The artists said their project was designed to help replace recently cut home-care services for the elderly by creating a "bank of exchange" at a local community center. For example, a carless senior might agree to offer the use of their kitchen to a college student in exchange for a ride to and from the grocery store. During my interview with Lowe, he said he and Ewald hoped their project would be "a practical vehicle that benefits people." I was stunned. Most of the creative artists and writers I interviewed for the paper focused on delivering information that would get their artwork seen and sold. Later that night, I researched Lowe and found a 2006 article in the *New York Times* that described the award-winning, Project Row Houses that Lowe had started in the early 1990s to help revitalize a run-down section of Houston.

Inspired by Lowe and Ewald's work, I remembered a PBS documentary that I had checked out of the library a few months earlier called *Healing Words*. It suggested a context for using my experience and skills as both a journalist and interdisciplinary artist. The film is about artists and writers at UF Health Shands Hospital's Arts in Medicine program in Gainesville, FL. In it, I saw Dr. John Graham Pole recite poetry he had written about his work as a pediatric oncologist. I saw dancer, Jill Sonke translate her medium of expression so that a patient confined to a hospital bed could perform with her.

These activities suggested a new way of dealing with illness. Rather than putting their lives on hold while they waited to recover, the film suggested that patients could continue to thrive creatively and even do activities that supported the healing process. It also suggested broader roles and contexts for artists to share common experiences in community. In the spring of 2010, with hopes of learning a new way of sharing my art practice with others, I proposed to do an internship with UF Health's Arts in Medicine program and enrolled in the University of Florida's Arts in Healthcare certificate program.

Clinical research, especially from the past couple of decades, suggests that a sort of holistic "healing" could result from patients' participation in creative processes. Rather than expecting an explicit physiological, psychological, or emotional outcome from a patient or caregiver, I sought to honor our shared humanity by offering the opportunity for creative expression. For many years, my personal writing and art practices have blended with my writer/artist-in-residence practice. I trained in a variety of artistic media, including creative writing, drawing, painting, and video production with the goal of being flexible so that I could help guide or participate with patients in as many creative activities as possible. During this time, my research and teaching have looked at the arts' historical and contemporary role in forming our ideas, conversations, and practices within health and science institutions and contexts. Today, I am also exploring how creativity intersects with other areas of our lives including education, aging, social justice, and parenting. Writing and reporting continue to help me understand my responsibilities to my community and not just my responsibility for myself.

ELIFETE PAZ

FIGURE 13.1: Elifete Paz. Image by Veronica Melendez.

1. A Happy Home

It's 2022. Two years after the start of the COVID-19 pandemic. I'm in the bathroom of my Ridgewood apartment in New York. A plastic shopping bag in the small, red waste bin is used for trash. It overfills too often. Considering it, something catches my eye: On the label of Mrs. Meyer's Clean Day hand soap is the line "Creating clean and happy homes since 2001." Even though the line makes no sense—How do you "create" a happy home? What does a "happy" home even look like?—I'm spooked. Something's in the bathroom with me. I'd think the bathroom was off-limits. But by now, I should expect no privacy from a perspective that would write such insidious lines like Mrs. Meyer's. Only a person of clear mind might shrug them off—my good friend Juan, for instance.

After living with Juan in his father's home during the 2020 quarantine, I've begun to admit to myself that I'm jealous of him. Although he's a better artist than I am, due in part to his clarity of mind, that's not why I'm jealous. It's more than that. He could be that rare bird: the truly happy. This doesn't mean he's nice. Another friend once asked how I could "stand" him. She made a face as if smelling sour milk, her lips puckered, nose wrinkled. And while he may disgust some people, what I am jealous of is his desire for nothing, nothing more or nothing different, from what he already has. Consider his father's home in the small village of Catskill, in Upstate New York. Most people desire something that surpasses mere survivability. Juan, on the other hand, seems undisturbed by his moldy, partially floundered home, content with one working bathroom Frankensteined with duct tape and machismo. "So it goes," I can imagine him saying as he hums along, literally, with potato chips in hand, attending his cherished collection of mugs, his cat, his dog, and a diabetic father. Honesty, a contentedness with what he has and who he is, defines Juan's happiness. I like to believe the same goes for me, but when it comes to being honest with myself, I lie all the time. And as a result, I am (for now) a failed writer sitting butt naked on a toilet in my Ridgewood apartment.

I began taking writing seriously here in New York City. I moved from West Texas in the summer of 2015. Before this, I wrote for a website that sold shitty photography equipment and even shittier photography-training ebooks. In New York, I was suddenly interning at Aperture Foundation, and I told myself I'd soon have bylines in the *New York Times* and *The New Yorker*, those stewards of good American English. Now, seven years later and nowhere near those goals, I'm in a bathroom putting unused toilet paper in a small, red waste bin to cover up a clump of my hair scrounged from the bathtub drain. Looking into the trash, I am facing a self-inflicted crisis: If I do lie all the time, what am I honest about? If I could, in reality, face myself, what would I see?

These are foundational questions I haven't yet answered in my writing. Answering them would require honesty. And even now I hesitate. I think instead of my mother, my grandmother, my childhood in Van Horn, Texas. For example, I learned the thing about putting toilet paper on top of my hair from my mother. I was convinced she taught all of us the same. But earlier this year, I asked my baby sister who lives with me if that was true, and not only did she deny it, but she also couldn't see why I wasted toilet paper. "You're 32, Freddy, there's no need to be ashamed of your hair." I hadn't considered shame. I thought it was natural to hide your fallen bits from prying eyes. I thought everybody did it to survive.

2. Pantomimus

Have I failed because I haven't written for the *New York Times* or *The New Yorker*? Of course not, it's even worse. It started in Van Horn, a small town (pop. 1893) in the middle of West Texas. It was the late 1990s, the Clinton years. September 11 hadn't happened. It was unimaginable. I had a best friend—let's call him Wallace—whose family was White and rich. Of course, Wallace's family wasn't rich, but to a 9-year-old Brown kid, living in a trailer park, now razed, on the poor side of town, middle class was rich. Did I mention his grandfather, Papaw, was the mayor? When I was with his family, I lorded over a swimming pool, and everything a young boy could ever want was in reach: unlimited Pokemon cards, the latest PlayStation videogames, and unedited Dragon Ball Z VHS tapes shipped straight from Japan. Back in our trailer, a rat could get stuck in the dryer and cook. At Wallace's, I watched *The Matrix* while eating stuffed crust pizza from Pizza Hut.

But there was a catch. We were rivals for distinction—victory was zero-sum. Only one of us could be the brightest, most gifted kid in fourth grade, and the motherfucker was smart enough to know I considered being Brown and poor a weakness. He'd happened upon unexploded ordnance. I remember one Van Horn summer (a Van Horn summer meant 100+ degrees) he refused to share water from his grandmother's outdoor spigot. We had just finished playing a home-run derby of sorts—I hit the baseball farther, faster, and more true than he ever could. I was thirsty. And he was a sore loser, blocking me from drinking water. It got to the point where I had to push him aside, and I did. We fought. Eventually, his grandmother, who I assume saw us from inside, came out and reprimanded both of us. Even before adulthood, I knew seeking friendship with White people may cause my own suffering.

Here's some honesty. Growing up in racist West Texas (where corporeal punishment for speaking Spanish was still allowed while my mother was in high school in the 1980s), I convinced myself I hated White people. For telling people I did, I apologize. Remember, I'm in a bathroom, looking at trash. I'm a failed writer (so far) because I haven't admitted to myself that I lied about hating White people. I don't. And this dishonesty has made me blind to the fact that I've been seeking their approval my whole life.

I spit out toothpaste from my mouth, as though prepping for an inquisition. Everything I've written before now was suited for the White gaze. I wrote lines like Mrs. Meyer's. And do you know how I "created" my happy homes? I refused to unmask the imagined reader in my mind. Like those Scooby-Doo villains, the person who hid under the monstrosity of my unexamined privileges—my US citizenship, my sex, my gender, my race—was a White man. The phone call, as they say, was coming from inside my home.

Within my home, without my body. If the voice of my imagined reader was the voice of a heteronormative, cis-gendered White American male, when I said I hated White people, did I actually mean I hated myself? I'm not White. I'm Brown. But the language I inherited shaped my consciousness. How do I see a world outside good American English?

My questions are not new. I remember Toni Morrison (1998), who confronted the White gaze head on, observed it's as if "[o]ur lives have no meaning, no depth without the white gaze. And I have spent my entire writing life trying to make sure that the white gaze was not the dominant one." After the election of

2016, I truly fear my entire life—all I am, all I've written, loved, cherished, hated—will finalize in violence. The White gaze of a White American male might be the last one to see my body in full, un-pixelated reality. I fear my last image will be censored, my face blurred, as seen in CCTV footage captured at the next Walmart a White American male terrorizes.

This is the gauntlet of writing true. Like the ancient Roman pantomimus, a silent performer of myths, who courted emperors and senators with his body and gesture, all the while masking his face, his tiniest, most delicate expressions, for their approval, I wore a mask of James Salter—or the self-exoticizing mask of Roberto Bolaño—my vestal virgins of Gérôme's *Pollice Verso*, the stewards of good American English. A thumbs up could signal deliverance. These masks may hide coarse elements. But even now, I hesitate. Honesty is too large for the size of me.

3. A Bathroom

Soft, slow light spills from a double-pane window three feet above the soapy, clouded water around his knees; glittered, multicolored clouds float there with him, and from one corner of the tub, he drops a Pantene Pro-V shampoo bottle into the water as he does to another brand of conditioner (Suave), while a Dove soap bar luxuriates on the corner beside the furthest and driest one from him, where he sees a hand towel, skewbald with bleach stains, folded crisply two times over from the middle, left there to use once the bather is ready to rejoin reality, the war is on (imagined between shampoo and conditioner battleships), and the tub water is tepid, so still at room temperature, filled nearly an hour ago by his grandmother. The door is closed, of course. He has privacy and peace. Yet, under the door, he can see a sliver of darkness, waiting to be let in.

A bathroom won't remember you. No matter how much your shit stinks. It doesn't care at all about how tired you are or how badly you sing. It actually cares less about why you cry or vomit. All the bathroom asks is, when you require it, you come freely. Its place in your home is where you face yourself naked. It's like what I imagine honesty to be.

If I'm honest, I'll probably never be happy like Juan. After 2020, I gave up writing art journalism. Two years later, I'm 32, and I have no idea where writing will take me now. But I can say this next phase of writing started with a journal, the first entry written while bedridden with COVID-19—"my hands have aged five years in a week, but that's also how time has felt." I was living with Juan because we both lost our jobs here in New York. In his father's home, he fed me eggplant Parmesan, eventually nursed me back to health. And when I was ready, we drank until we were shit faced. We had unemployment money and all the time in the world. Maybe this is my own instance of a happy home? From here, I published an essay entitled "A Violence and Gentleness of Wind," and now I'm writing poems about the bathroom.

I hope some of my poems take the stupid form of litany: "Oh, Pine-Sol, Scrubbing Bubbles, Windex, and Draino, and you Irish Spring, Colgate and Crest, the Pepto-Bismol." But I will make most of these small, incidental. They're my first steps outside a White gaze, even if I suspect that's impossible in English.

I am washing my hands now. I am opening the door. I begin to walk down the hallway painted the same red as my grandmother's kitchen floor. Back behind me is the bathroom, gleaming after its use—where I leave behind Mrs. Meyer's, all I've written before—my home still unaware of the transformation, the chemistry performed on its behalf by the bathroom.

This is me as a writer right now.

Reference

Morrison, Toni, (1998), Toni Morrion interview with Charlie Rose, https://charlierose.com/videos/17664. Accessed September 18, 2024.

GLENN ADAMSON

FIGURE 14.1: Glenn Adamson. Image by John Michael Kohler Arts Center.

Talking to Artists

I AM OFTEN asked what, exactly, I do for a living. And the answer makes me feel vaguely guilty. I'm one of those "can't-do-teach" types. I suppose a lot of art critics and historians could say the same. Like me, maybe they even started out wanting to be artists themselves, before realizing they weren't cut out for it. But I think my "can't do-ness" is worse than most, as I am mainly a specialist in craft. I write about people with deep skills, who have usually spent years developing them. In fact, I've published many books on that topic, some criticism, a few theoretical pieces, and even co-founded a scholarly journal. All without really knowing what it is to make something by hand, with complete and consummate control.

What I can do is write. This gives me, I suppose, a vicarious sense of involvement in the artist's creative life, which is what really sets my imagination on fire. For me, this activity begins at home, as my partner Nicola Stephanie is herself an artist. When I met her in London, she was mainly a filmmaker; now, her work takes the form of constructions at the midpoint of painting and sculpture. Seeing this transition up close, and vicariously experiencing the ups and downs, ins and outs of her practice, has been as transformative an education as graduate school. My relationship with Nicola has only deepened the fascination I have long held about artists' experience. Jackson Pollock once said, "Technique is just a means of arriving at a statement" (Namuth and Paul Falkenberg [1951] 2013). I take a nearly opposite viewpoint: For me, the artwork is significant primarily as a doorway which leads back into the passage of its own creation. That process is invariably an unstable and reactive compound of thinking and making.

All of this helps to explain, maybe, why what I love best about my job is talking to artists. This is fundamentally why I care about craft. It is the feedback system between an artist and their own work, the means by which their capabilities are tested and their ideas manifested. When I ask an artist *how* they make a work, what I'm really doing is asking to be let into that world of possibilities, a world like the one I once hoped to build for myself. From this perspective, it's hard to understand how craft came to be an object of disregard by so many in the art world. Explaining why that was too long the case—suffice to say, it has a lot to do with sexism and racism—was a major preoccupation of my early work. In any case, the disdain has ebbed in recent years. Today, when I talk to artists, they are usually happy to talk about matters of technique. And that in turn often leads to the most interesting conceptual terrain.

But let me take a step back, because I haven't yet said what I mean by "talking to artists." There are many varieties of this experience, ranging from boozy late-night speculation to formal in-gallery presentation. All can be enlightening. What I mainly want to address here, though, is the process of interviewing an artist specifically in order to write about their work. I do this all the time. And this in itself positions me in a certain way. There is a school of thought that a writer should approach an artist "cold"—a revealing way of putting it, as it implies not just independence and objectivity, but also a lack of emotional investment. Again, I would take a nearly opposite viewpoint. Unless I am working up an exhibition review (which is the least rewarding kind of writing I do), I always prefer to speak to an artist before setting down a word. Typically, I also ask them to review what I have written at the draft stage, to make corrections and suggestions.

There is nothing unusual about this method—most art writers probably do the same—but it contains within it certain commitments which seem worthy of reflection. First and most obviously, using this method implies that I am an ally. Artists—apart from those few operating at the uppermost tier of the market—have it tough. Theirs is a precarious job, poorly remunerated. It typically requires workspace, tools and materials, and training, all of which are getting more expensive all the time, particularly in New York City (where I live) and in other art world centers. The vocation also calls for a rare combination of vulnerability, i.e., the willingness to expose one's deepest thoughts and feelings in public, and a degree of strategic cunning. The demands are high. Artists may not need champions. In my experience, they are remarkably self-sufficient—but they certainly deserve them.

Furthermore, the discursive context in which artworks now land is comparatively weak. It has not grown in tandem with the expansion of the art market, or the institutional infrastructure of galleries, fairs, and museums. Back in the 1960s, there were relatively few professional artists and a very robust critical apparatus. Today the situation is reversed. It is quite possible for an artist to become moderately successful without having anything of real intellectual merit published on their work. This situation has led me to consider artists to be the first and best audience for whatever I may write about them. What I'm looking for, usually, is not to surprise them with a novel interpretation—a new insight into what they have been doing—but rather to give them a feeling of being understood. I once curated an exhibition about the Toronto-based artist Gord Peteran; he joked that his job was to fire an arrow in the air, and mine was to plant it in a target of my choice. I thought that was pretty funny, but it doesn't actually describe what I try to do. When I send a draft text to an artist, the ideal response is not "How interesting, I never thought of that"; but "At last, somebody gets it."

This raises an obvious question. What am I doing on the artist's behalf that they could not do for themselves? Of course, many artists simply aren't skilled writers, any more than I am a skilled sculptor. So that's something. But I think more important is the fact that an artist's writing on their own work has a special status, whether they like it or not. The phrase "artist's statement" is used for a reason. Anything written by an artist is necessarily taken as a self-conscious assertion of purpose—if not actually a constituent element of their work, then an immediate adjunct to it. In academic parlance, it is a "primary text." Even if intended or expressed as opinion or interpretation, it will be treated as fact. A critic's writing, by contrast, is "secondary," distanced not by virtue of some artificial objective stance, but simply through the shift of voice. An artist's statement is a message sent to the world. A critic's writing signals that the message has been received. My goal is, above all, to ensure the clarity of the transmission.

All of this has a bearing on how I talk to artists. I am not a big believer in the significance of the revealing aside—the little thing, the throwaway line, that is supposedly a tipoff to what is "really" going on in the work. Conversational detail might help embroider the tale, but it is not going to be the whole story. It might even distract from the main goal, which is to capture exactly what the artist intends. This skill is one that I've tried to develop over the years. It involves not just open-mindedness, which is a prerequisite, but also knowledge of many kinds: technical, historical, and theoretical. Miss the first reference, and you may not be offered a second. A writer must be ready to receive anything an artist tries to give—and it is a gift, an artist's deepest thinking.

I ask questions too, of course. These mostly follow the classic oral historian's technique: repeat what you have just heard, but in interrogative form. If an artist says (as one did to me, recently) that she feels "a little guilty" about her current work, the only reply I can imagine is: "why guilty?" The goal is to keep the conversation in that place, until the artist has said what they need to say. I also pose other sorts of questions. Given my interest in craft, I frequently ask about technique, but always starting with *why*, not *how*. The objective is to understand how the bridge from process to idea is constructed. Similarly, I may ask about a possible reference point: "Were you thinking about Helen Frankenthaler when you made this?" The intention here is not to deflect the conversation into art history, but to establish how the artist positions themselves.

As is probably clear by now, my idea of good critical writing is not writing about the critic. If I wanted to make the same arguments over and over, I wouldn't need to talk to artists at all. The whole point is to learn from them, and help others to do the same. In this respect, I am consciously departing from a trajectory of art writing that emerged in the intellectual forge of modernism, and carried on through the late twentieth century. Within that tradition, critics staked out positions and then chose artists who exemplified them. I can understand the power of this approach, but can't really identify with it. The reasons I agree to write about particular artists are very different, and somewhat complicated. My colleague Julia Bryan-Wilson had it right when she told me that (a) you make your career on what you say "no" to; and (b) there are three possible reasons you might say "yes": money (the gig pays well), status (it will be high profile), and friendship (you want to help out). Her advice was to take things on only when two of these three boxes could be ticked. Julia is surely right about this, but there is also another consideration, which tends to be more decisive in my experience: Do I feel like I'm the right person? Do I feel an affinity to the artist, that is, and do I know enough to do a good job? My choice of subjects may imply that I am on a mission—in my case, to set out an expansive context for thinking through craft. That has an element of truth, but it's really more a matter of competency.

Talk to enough artists, and they get to be friends as well as allies. This raises a final point, which concerns duration. It may seem a little counterintuitive, given everything I've said thus far, but a critic's writing on an artist does not necessarily improve with age. Prolonged exposure, over a period of years, just results in a different thing—less like a stir fry, more like a stew. The initial impact of an artist's ideas can be bracing, and it's exciting to capture that energy in a piece of writing. Equally, it is gratifying to observe an artist slowly, surely, change their mind. This is what we all do in life; artists are among the few whose evolution is a matter of disciplinary interest. This is the implicit subject matter of any retrospective exhibition. And it is one more reason for the critic to prize receptivity. If you care about an artist, you probably care about them young, old, and in-between. The late work does not contradict the early.

In this respect, as in so many others, the writer's relationship to an artist is ideally not one of judgment, or self-interest, or manifesto mongering. As I finish this essay, in fact, I realize I have given it the wrong title. Because good art writing is not a matter of talking at all. It's a matter of listening.

Reference

Namuth, Hans and Falkenberg, Paul (prods) ([1951] 2013), *Jackson Pollock 51*, film excerpt, Seattle: University of Washington Libraries Media Center.

HAKIM BISHARA

FIGURE 15.1: Hakim Bishara. Image by Steel Stillman.

IT WAS A week before rent was due, and I didn't have the money to pay it. The situation was dire: I'd already borrowed all the money that I could borrow, maxed out three credit cards, and used up a small bank loan. My savings were long gone. There were no safety nets left. And paying the rent late again was out of the question.

My head was boiling with anxiety and my legs were tapping uncontrollably as I crunched the numbers: The rent was $1200 but all I had in my account was $100 for one article that had taken over a week to write. I was expecting another $800 from an acting gig in an art film about the refugee crisis in Europe.

For two weeks I had played the character of an Iraqi refugee who wanders through a fictional no-man's-land with his only friend, a fake caged bird. I was cast for the role not for my acting skills, but because my Middle Eastern features fit the typecast. The character was an esoteric poet who had a special interest in astrophysics, particularly black holes. I had to memorize a long monologue about the mysteries of matter and anti-matter and perform it on camera while dressed up in rags with dirt smeared all over my face. I later heard that the video was shown at the *Lyon Biennale* in France, where it received raving reviews. I was never invited to the debut. Instead, I was writing desperate emails to the producer, begging to be paid immediately. I also tried to convince her to pay me the "leading actor" price of $1000, but she reminded me that I wasn't part of the actor's union. She did promise, however, to wire me the $800 before the end of the month.

I wasn't sure whether I could believe her, but I decided to take her word for it and focus on getting those remaining $300.

I'd already minimized my meals to rice and chickpeas and reduced all other expenses to the bare minimum. Month after month, my life ambitions had been reduced to the mere privilege of affording to pay my rent and basic bills. As this struggle kept repeating itself, I'd started to slowly give up on the dream of sustaining a life in New York City.

I gave myself a deadline: If I don't get a steady job, any job, in the next four months, I'll give up and go back home.

But going back home would mean accepting the greatest failure of my life.

Coming to New York had been my shot at a second chance. Home was, and still is, a hostile environment for me and people like me: Palestinians who have homes within the state of Israel.

Our story is unknown to most people, so I'll give a brief historical explanation here: There are about two million Palestinians in Israel today—we're the few whose families weren't killed or expelled from their homes during the war of 1948, which ended with the establishment of the state of Israel. In the mid-1960s, after living for about 20 years under martial law in heavily guarded ghettos, we were cut off from our relatives in the West Bank and Gaza and given Israeli citizenship. They call us "Arab Israelis." Meanwhile, the newborn state of Israel confiscated most of my family's lands, turning us from landowners to low-waged factory workers. My small hometown, which is only a 30-miute drive from Tel Aviv, is now surrounded by a ring of lavish Israeli settlements that were built on our lands. I had to see them every time I looked out the windows of my parents' house.

To cut a long story short, we became second-class citizens, discriminated in every area of life and perpetually suspected to be a fifth column. There was no chance for me and my friends to live a life of dignity in that place. Everyone I know who had a chance to leave did. And in the fall of 2015, at age 36, my chance finally arrived.

I was sitting with friends in a café in Tel Aviv, drinking tequila shots and recycling bad political jokes when my friend Eyal called me saying: "You just hit the lottery!" He told me there was an "art writing" MFA program in New York that had one last spot left, and that they were willing to give a scholarship to the right candidate.

I laughed and reminded him of a slight hitch—that I'd never finished my bachelor's degree. In the last year of my studies at the Hebrew University in Jerusalem in the early aughts, attacks and counterattacks between Palestinians and Israelis escalated so much that life in the city had become unbearable. I was stopped and frisked every time I left my house, especially if I had a stubbled face. I remember testing the risk element of beard growing: a freshly shaven faced helped me go almost undetected, but a two-day stubble or more meant a high chance of being shoved into the back of a police car and detained. Those were the years of the Second Intifada, or Palestinian uprising. I slipped into a life of hedonism and dark cynicism, fueled by drugs and alcohol. Campus looked and felt like an army base with barbed wire fences and professors preaching "enlightened Zionism." I eventually dropped out and never returned, though I only had a few courses left to earn my diploma.

"How on earth would I sustain a life in New York?" I screamed into the phone at Eyal. "I'm not much of a critic either. You're crazy!" It's not that I hadn't fantasized about getting the hell out of Israel. But my only dreams of exile up to that point had been limited to Europe—Berlin, London, Paris—where I'd done a few stints, staying each time until my money ran out. "How on earth would I sustain a life in New York?" I asked again, this time to my friends at the bar.

"Listen," one of them answered, "if you don't leave now, you'll never get out. This chance isn't going to come a second time."

I had to quickly throw together an application. I wasn't writing much at the time. After working for different media outlets in Israel for 15 years, writing mostly in Hebrew, I was sick of being the go-to, sardonic, token Palestinian voice for lefty Israeli publications. I had decided to quit and become an artist. But before I got there, I made a few detours. My most recent job had been working in an online casino. That was the only place that would give me a full-time job because they needed an Arabic speaker to lure filthy-rich gambling sheikhs from the Gulf into the game. But since the operation was held in Tel Aviv, it was a job requirement to assume an alias—mine was a Palestinian student living in Sofia, Bulgaria, working hard to fund his studies. I ended up building personal relationships with the gamblers, without them ever knowing who I really was. In long phone calls and online chats during night shifts, they told me about their marriage problems, or the headaches of yacht repair. I gained their trust by actively discouraging them from continuing to play, explaining in detail how rigged the game was.

The Israeli media, like the rest of society, was getting increasingly jingoistic. There was a dichotomy in the way that Israelis perceived me as a Palestinian in their midst: I was either fetishized by the few remaining leftists who so dearly wanted a Palestinian friend, or demonized by nationalists who so dearly wanted me dead. There weren't many hues in between. Working as an online casino dealer under a pseudonym offered more dignity.

Less than a month later, I was in New York studying in the MFA program, which had miraculously accepted me based on writing experience in place of an undergrad degree. All the money I came with evaporated within one year of living in New York. My family helped in the second year of my studies because they were so eager to see me hold any sort of diploma. When I finally received the cherished piece of paper they'd been waiting for over 15 years, they framed it and hung it in their living room. The following year—the gap year allowed by my student visa for "professional training"—I tried to make a living as a freelance writer. That's when the hand-to-mouth lifestyle began, bringing us back to those $300 that I needed to get my hands on.

I started rummaging through my few belongings, which could all be fit into one suitcase, to see what I could sell, but I found nothing anyone would want to buy. I then resorted to the "Gigs" section on Craigslist, where I'd found that acting stint in the art film.

I tried to be strategic with my hunt, knowing that any good job opening in New York would have thousands of more qualified candidates, so I limited my search to jobs for Arabic speakers. That yielded some unorthodox results.

There were a few interpretation jobs for the CIA, but you had to be an American citizen to apply. There were also some teaching jobs, but I had no experience, and the selection process would take too long. But then I drifted into a miscellaneous category where the services of an Arabic speaker were needed for entirely different purposes.

I opened an ad posted by a man who identified as white and middle-aged, seeking an Arabic-speaking male to "dominate and humiliate him" while he would "crawl naked across the floor."

I entertained the idea for a moment. But I soon realized that the guy was probably an Iraq vet working through his PTSD, atoning for anything on his conscience through this power reversal, with a dose of BDSM for good measure.

Then there was another man, also white, who wrote that he was looking for an Arab man for whom he could cross-dress as a "Muslim wife," headscarf and all, and perform chores like cooking and cleaning. He noted that his fantasy originated out of a deep "respect for Islam." Best part—he'd pay *you* to do *your* housework! Somehow this ad disturbed me even more than the other one.

Next, I tried Hebrew. After sifting through a dozen nanny jobs for Israeli expat families, I landed on an opening for a line cook job at a Hasidic Chinese restaurant in Brooklyn.

The idea of a Kosher Chinese restaurant run by Hasids fascinated me. I'd never seen a Hasidic Chinese restaurant in Israel. The multiculturalism of the United States must have seeped into this hermetic community after all, I thought. Besides, I'd never worked at a restaurant and had always felt that I would be punished for not going through this humbling experience. So I decided to call the number in the ad. The owner, a man named Moishe, answered the phone.

"What experience do you have in restaurant work?" Moishe asked in a thick Yiddish accent. "None," I replied.

He sighed and said, "Okay, well, we need someone quick. Come for an interview tomorrow."

The restaurant was located deep into Crown Heights. Inside, families with multiple children were dining on Kosher Lo Mein and sweet-and-sour chicken. When I walked in, all heads turned to figure out who the goy was. Their eyes looked me up and down. I was just as captivated by them.

Moishe—a disheveled, relatively young, and slightly overweight man—had a little office, the size of a closet, behind the kitchen. It was squalid, and so small that I couldn't even enter after him. He sat at his tiny desk and I stood in the doorway. He wiped his sweaty forehead and asked me how I spoke Hebrew. I told him I was born near Tel Aviv.

"What's your name again?"

"Hakim."

The jig was up. He pulled on his beard and readjusted his yarmulke. I gave him a wide smile and explained that I was Palestinian. He took a moment to process that information.

"So you're a Palestinian Jew who was there before the state of Israel?"

"No, just a Palestinian."

"But you lived in Israel?"

"Technically, yes," I said.

"And your nationality?"

"Technically, Israeli."

Moishe, who spoke Yiddish and English, knew only a few words in Hebrew. I wondered why he'd put an ad out for a Hebrew speaker and figured it was just a sort of test of "character." Hasidic Jews in New York are often anti-Zionists, actually (according to the Torah, the Jews shall not return to the land of Israel before the arrival of the Messiah), but not Moishe. He was downright obsessed with the place. He had a million questions for me. "How is the weather in Jerusalem this time of year?" "How busy is it at the Wailing Wall after dark?" etc. I impressed him with my knowledge.

He had one more reservation: "Are you sure this is for you? I don't know if you'll last here for long, but you can try."

I smiled, guiltily. In my head I'd already worked it all out: I'd be a line cook for Moishe for exactly one week, just long enough to get those $300, and then quit.

"I've been wanting to gain some restaurant experience, actually," I told him. "I'm saving up to visit the Holy Land." His eyes lit up again. We came to an agreement that I'd work until he found someone to fill the position permanently.

I realized it was Friday, just before the Sabbath started, and so I wouldn't begin until after the day of rest, Sunday. That took two days off my plan! Now I had only five to make enough money to pay my rent.

On my way back to the subway, I burst out laughing and patted myself on the shoulder for stepping into another interesting unknown. But a sadness quickly settled in. I'd come to New York to start a new life and fulfill my dream of becoming an accomplished writer, not chop onions for another Zionist!

I'd known as soon as I walked out the place that I wouldn't tell anyone about this. I would certainly not be telling my girlfriend, who'd already lent me too much money, and who was worried in general about my future in this country. This was my humiliating secret.

At 7:00 a.m. the next morning, I was at the restaurant to start my first day of work. The job was to prepare ingredients for the chefs, who were Chinese, and who generally gave me the stink eye. And rightly so. I was terrible at everything. Especially chopping onions. Moishe had to teach me how to do it the right way (cut the stems first). By the end of the day I reeked like onions and had cuts all over my hands.

Moishe paid $12 per hour, but the number of work hours every day was not fixed. It depended on how busy the restaurant was. Every time I got a short break, I'd run outside to inhale a cigarette and calculate how much I'd earned. The second day, when I was given my ten minutes, I called my girlfriend, pretending to be out for a stroll.

"You're strolling?" she asked.

"Well, and, you know, looking for a job. But also strolling."

"It's raining!"

It took four days of toil to put together $200. And on the fifth day, Moishe told me he'd found a permanent replacement.

"You know this is not for you," he said. "*Nachon*!" I replied in Hebrew—"True!"

He was a nice guy, that Moishe.

Exhausted, hands bloodied, head bowed, I walked home. But somehow the relief of not having to work there anymore was almost euphoric—I was smiling as I walked down the street, even as I realized that coming up with $100 in an afternoon was likely impossible. There was that suspended moment of tranquility before you fall into the abyss. I still wasn't sure if that wire transfer from the producer was even going to come through.

I passed out from anxiety and exhaustion as soon as I got home, but I awoke in a panic at 3:00 a.m. I opened my laptop to do what I'd been too scared to do all day: check my bank account to see if the acting money had come through. Sure enough, it was there, and to my surprise, the producer had given in and paid me $1000 instead of $800. So, there I was, a rich man: Not only could I pay my rent, but I also had $100 to spare. The next evening, I took my girlfriend out for Chinese food—but not in Crown Heights.

HRAG VARTANIAN

FIGURE 16.1: Hrag Vartanian. Image by Rowan Renee.

I REMEMBER THE first time I met Ara Baliozian, a portly Armenian Canadian author. He had traveled from his small Ontario town to the Armenian cultural center in what was at the time the city of Scarborough, today the eastern part of Toronto. It was 1991, and he was wearing clothes that looked like the most affordable he could buy on a limited budget. I was terrified meeting this person whose mind was splayed on every page and who had provided me with a clear view of the world through his eyes. I don't remember much else from that meeting except feeling shy and reserved. I didn't know what to ask him. I felt like someone had conjured up a spirit in front of me, and I just remember looking perplexed and in awe.

He was the first "author" I had met whose books I had read, the first who lived off the craft of writing, scribbling words for a panoply of publications, each more curious to me than the next. His mostly slim books—which I figured out years later, were almost entirely self-published—provided me insight into what it meant to be a diasporan artist by writing commentary in community newspapers, books of translation, small volumes of maxims and observations, and short stories, poems, and anything else he could get published. I'd gleaned from his writing that it was mostly a joyless job, tinged with anger, alienation, and flashes of wisdom. Through his books I realized that to write in and for a diaspora was to write for an audience that might not exist in the future. It was a consciousness negotiated daily for a readership always on the verge of disappearing. Our precarity as a community of diasporan Armenians spread around the globe is a feature, not a liminal state.

I discovered his books through the executive director of the center, Salpi Der Ghazarian, who took a liking to me and would squirrel away notable books when they arrived, knowing I'd consume them as quickly as the kebabs, *kuftes*, and pilaf that were a draw at community gatherings and attracted far more interest than book readings and other cultural events ever would. Ara once poked at that sad reality in one of his books: "What's the difference between an Armenian cultural center and yogurt? There's more culture in yogurt."

I slept with Ara's books in my room; sometimes they were in my bed, under the covers with me, or folded by my pillow since I had fallen asleep reading them. I read and reread them in my teen years. Sometimes on the subway, the bus, or in the backseat of my parents' car, providing comfort, like some sort of talisman. They became part of my life in a way few things did. I started a correspondence with him but I found it intimidating. I wrote him letters with a typewriter, and he always wrote back, often flourishing the pages with little pen doodles of his bespectacled face. He was encouraging, telling me to stop being self-deprecating, that my writing was more than "good enough." Looking back I can see my youthful prose was malformed, but it certainly wasn't as bad as my childhood shame made me believe. I prized those letters, too. One day, I thought, I could be a writer.

In the final years of high school, I joined a group of other youthful Armenian Canadians to publish *Aysor*, an English-language publication that we printed cheaply and distributed to the community at large. Salpi, again, herded us together, and we decided to organize an inaugural public event. Someone suggested Ara as a speaker and I enthusiastically endorsed the idea. We reached out to him to see if he'd come. He said he didn't drive, which was surprising considering he lived in a remote place many of us snobbish Torontonians called "the armpit of Ontario." It was only 113 km (79 miles) away so we offered to drive him to and from, but he refused. We were perplexed. "I refuse to partake in your generosity," he said. "Once a writer gets used to the wining and dining of the rich benefactors and cultural patrons, they come to expect it."

It was surprising, even if incredibly noble to some of us who were still figuring out how we wanted to exist in the world. I remember feeling crushed at the news, thinking it would be wonderful to toast him in a room of people gazing at him adoringly. Yet, in retrospect, I think that advice was more valuable than anything he could've said by visiting us.

During college, I probably learned less about writing than I should've, but I quickly realized how networks assured some people's voices were heard over others. The main literary program on Toronto television at the time was hosted by Daniel Richler, son of one of the grandfathers of contemporary Canadian literature, Mordecai Richler. He was a pretty good host, not great, and it was clear to many of us who watched how he got all his breaks. I remember standing in line at a bookstore to have my copy of Richler's father's new book *Jerusalem* signed. I waited patiently until I got to the front and he asked my name. I shyly told him and spelled it out, as I'm used to doing. "What is it?" he asked, like it was a specimen in a petri dish. "Armenian," I said. "Did you write about the Armenian Quarter of Jerusalem?" I asked, hoping he would whet my appetite for his book. "No, I didn't; are you from there?" he asked coldly. "No, but I know some who are," I offered, thinking he might be interested, and remembering Salpi herself was. He quickly dismissed me, as if I was in the way of his fame.

I felt sad as I wondered how he sidestepped a quarter of the Old City. I never ended up reading the book, though I lugged it with me to every apartment I lived in until I sold it in 2008 on Amazon, finally accepting that I was never going to wander its pages, knowing it had circumvented a whole part of the city that I was most curious about. Only when writing this essay did I discover that same book that I'd mailed 16 years ago in a box full of unopened mail, but this time with "Return to Sender" scrawled on the manila packet. Sometimes books aren't done with us.

I was quickly learning that the job of being a writer is not only their words but also how the writer lives and moves in the world. It is also about how they correspond and with whom, and while there are always exceptions to the norm, the reality is that writers reflect the culture they uphold or wrestle to change. Both Baliozian and Richler couldn't diverge from their paths, but with very different reasons. The former did so to ensure his critical insights were never tempered, while the latter couldn't be bothered to move past mainstream media narratives for which his adoring public was hungry. I saw how fame could warp a writer's work until they dismissed a young, eager reader who spent over an hour on a bus each way to attend a talk and buy a book.

Years later, I sent Ara an illuminated version of his short story "The Greek Poetess," using collage, ink, and paint—it was my only copy. He sent it back. "I can't accept this kind gift," he wrote in reply, admitting he didn't understand modern or contemporary art and saying that I should keep it, that he was undeserving. Again, he refused to have his ego stroked.

If books are the fuel of writing, it is a sense of place that often shapes the vessel for those thoughts. The writers in my literary cosmos were more often than not from places I'd never been but they'd allow me to walk through other lands using my imagination.

When I arrived in Beirut in 1997 to work at Haigazian University, I didn't feel welcome until I read Etel Adnan's *Of Cities and Women*. In this thin volume, I learned that writing can soothe the felt alienation of a new home. Her description was so accurate, lyrical, and inviting that it opened up Beirut for me even when she described the Mediterranean metropolis as being the color of diarrhea or metaphorically talked about the cruel realities of a place that can tear at your skin with its contradictions and injustice. Decades later, I discovered my husband's uncles were friends with Adnan and her partner before the Lebanese Civil War, and while they knew she was a writer, they had no idea she was also an artist or that she was anybody of great renown. "She never told you?" I asked. "No, they were just Etel and Simone," Uncle Henri explained, pointing out their comfortable friendship with two people who many people see as one of Lebanon's most renowned artistic couples.

In the Lebanese capital, I learned that writers can write in obscurity, witnessing and recording events that rocked them to the core, but at the edge of empire it was mostly unnoticed. I shared meals with students, as the college's director of student publications, and heard shocking stories about a war that had only ended seven years before—and I'd often be the only one at the table who would pause at the horror of finding dead bodies hanging from lamp posts on the way home. I still remember the student who couldn't finish his article for the college newspaper because the man in the apartment upstairs was beating his wife all night. "Why didn't you call the police?" I said before he looked at me like I was from Mars and walked away.

I wanted to tell these stories but in some ways they weren't mine to tell. None of the students wanted to write them down either, preferring to regurgitate the same expected tales about food, cultural observations about faraway places, or fantasy fiction, as their imagination was the only space where they could be free. I quickly learned the importance of freedom for a writer. As much as my imagination felt alive in that city, my passport shielded me from the realities of a place that was deeply sectarian and doled out justice based on your connections, or *wasta*, a complicated term that has no English equivalent.

Writers, I'd learn again and again, never really work alone, we are deeply social and connected to the world, even if we don't want to admit it. As it happens, those writers who wrote from what seemed to my teenage self to be far-off locales, like Paul Bowles in Morocco, Joseph Conrad in Congo, James Baldwin in Istanbul, or Montesquieu in Isfahan, were connected to networks elsewhere that circulated their words. Writing could be truth or lies, but someone else's words could also be the beginning of your own story.

In the 1990s, moving from Toronto to Beirut, before landing in New York City, where I live now, I don't know if I was really conscious of how I would support myself as a writer, since zine culture was at its zenith and in my circles the handmade and wonky was often more celebrated than the polished work appearing in books produced by corporate publishers. Though I never thought that I needed someone else's permission, I grew up in a community that supported artists badly, and when almost any books of Armenian interest were published, a small group of us, mostly the same few dozen people, would gather to buy copies and listen to the author dutifully, regardless whether the topic interested us. Most of those purchased copies remain unread.

My own parents were not a fan of the idea of me being any type of writer or artist. My dad's second-grade education meant he read slowly and with trouble in any of the four languages he could fudge his way through, even though his father Setrag was reputedly a prolific scribe. My grandfather wrote letters for others in Armenian and Ottoman Turkish with Armenian letters, a common practice as the people in the Ottoman Empire often retained their native alphabet even when they wrote in a foreign language. He never properly learned Arabic after the Armenian Genocide when he was forced into a refugee camp in Aleppo. And after a truck accident in the 1950s, my grandfather was bedridden where he shriveled away until he died a few years before I was born. After the genocide, Turkish made an abrupt turn and adopted the Latin script instead of Arabic letters, while the Armenian language he knew was not used in Syria for official correspondence. So, my grandfather's writing talent was functionally useless in the world he inhabited as a refugee. Even Ara Baliozian, who started his career dreaming of writing in Armenian, had to eventually adopt English to make some semblance of a living. That agility, I learned, was necessary for a writer in diaspora to live. My maternal grandfather, who spoke six languages with varying levels of accuracy, used to love saying, "When you learn someone else's language, they don't conquer you, you conquer them."

My father remembers his father writing his own genocide story in a small book, which he promised my dad he'd let him and his siblings read after he died. At the funeral, my grandmother slipped the book into the coffin and my dad and his siblings never learned his harrowing story, which included the massacre of his first family. In the late 1990s, I shared this story with my father's sister, who didn't remember such a thing. She asked a friend to open the coffin to see if it did indeed exist and when the woman lifted the lid she said there was a book-like form that crumbled into dust as soon as she tried to touch it. All that remains is a shadow of his story. Writing is fragile. It needs a reader to embrace it and protect it in order to exist.

In her own role, my mother taught me about the importance of readers. Growing up she was always glued to the *Toronto Star*, which she read religiously. Stacks of newspapers that would stain your fingers with ink accumulated in the corners of our home. I'd pore over the pages as well, but they also were a source of irritation to my younger self. My mother was often buried in those pages when I wanted her to look at me, hungry for her attention.

In retrospect, I figured out the black letters on the newsprint were her balm for a toxic marriage, but in those years I thought the long, crumpled pages must have been more interesting than me. It was a strange thing to wrestle with for a young kid, but it pushed me to grapple with what writing "did" for its audience. Through the *Star*, my mother learned about the world around us, including how to "become" a Canadian. She also learned that women could demand things, that LGBTQ+ people existed, what race was, and how it worked in society. She wasn't allowed to pursue the education she once dreamt of but she was able to be in dialogue with a world bigger than her life in Rexdale.

In late 1990s Beirut, I knew I was already becoming a writer, but I wasn't sure exactly what kind. By the end of the century I'd moved to New York City for a nonprofit job at the Armenian General Benevolent Union. I assumed the majority of writers held other jobs, while doing their own writing in their private time. I never imagined a queer, Syrian Armenian, Canadian kid would find a place in the publishing world that could sustain my life financially, so from the beginning I always expected I'd be forced to do something else, though never knowing what that might or could be.

My first decade in New York was one of the most difficult and exhilarating times of my life. I worked at an organization that allowed me to pen articles for their publications in addition to humdrum press releases and promotional fodder. I smoked a lot, jogged regularly, clubbed five nights a week, and lived with a man I'd eventually fall in love with, though it destroyed our friendship. I call these my "Zero Years" as I had the ridiculous idea that we, as humans, should leave no trace. I was committed to living my art and creating writing that would disappear. I would scrawl things on paper, or sometimes metal poles while I waited for a bus, or on found newspapers, leaving my words for whoever would find them. Writing, I thought, should be mostly ephemeral. This, of course, means that I don't have a lot of unpublished writing from that period. It was also a time when I was placed in a surveillance program post-9/11 as a Middle-Eastern-born male on a work visa. Fifteen years later the government did it again, but this time the mostly US-based media branded it the "Muslim Registry," which would eventually spark popular outrage.

Later, I met the man who would become my husband, Veken Gueyikian, and he wanted to be supportive of my work. He introduced me to blogging and he convinced me of its importance.

One day he asked if I wanted to write a book. "Sure," I said, perplexed about the relationship between the two. "Who do you think is going to read it?" he asked. "People interested in the topic?" I replied.

He looked at me with sweet eyes and explained that the world didn't work that way, adding that if I blogged I could build an audience—even if it was a few dozen people—who would one day buy my book.

My naivety was palpable, but thankfully I was smart enough to listen to him. That early experiment in building a readership helped me find my passion for online writing, and I quickly became obsessed. The relationship I, as an online writer, have with my audience feels important, invigorating, and part of me can't help but wonder if the little kid in me trying to get his mom's attention isn't also part of the mix.

Financially I had my day job, but I was writing for other places, including the *Brooklyn Rail*, a publication that never paid its writers at the time because of their terrible nonprofit model. But I used that time to develop my voice, feeling free to write and publish what I wanted without the stress of making a living.

In 2009, Veken and I were newly married. The world had financially collapsed just the year before, and we were itching to do something to shake ourselves out of the humdrum of dead-end gigs. Veken had squirreled away some money during his years in the closet working in digital strategy and marketing, and I had a job that ensured our health care and a stable income. We decided to try to launch our own website, named *Hyperallergic*, which would work to pay writers and engage with political topics around art they felt were important. Having gone to college in the 1990s, I saw the culture wars waging south of the border and felt frustrated with the lack of art media addressing these issues in an honest, loving, critical, and immediate way, as opposed to the watered-down stereotypes we read in corporate media outlets. My experience is also deeply informed by my registry in the NSEERS surveillance program, when I learned how the media could be silent when faced with the racialized horror of governmental bigotry. At that time, no one ran to the airports to protest, or penned opinion pieces to stop the registry, or ranted in public that we should not be forced to endure this insanity. Every day I felt the very real possibility that I could disappear at a moment's notice. I also grew up in a community whose genocide was not recognized by society at large, so I knew that no one would tell our stories, and ultimately we had to tell them ourselves.

Veken and I started with a $3500 investment of our own money, and worked night and day—not always writing what I wanted but what we had to in order to compete in the marketplace and build a platform for the conversations we actually wanted to have. Veken, who has advanced degrees, felt alienated and uninterested in the articles circulating in the art trade media at the time. We looked to blogging models in politics, tech, and other fields for inspiration. We paid ourselves nothing for the first four years, then a token salary for many years thereafter. Our first employee, and subsequent employees, were paid far more. We slowly increased our payments to writers from an initial amount of $15 to the $250 to $500 we offer for most articles today, more than some other publications, which feels good.

Only recently have I been able to write what I initially wanted to, though I've also written and published a great deal of other work along the way. I learned to write quickly, enjoying the thrill of tapping out characters at what can feel like the speed of light, learning to microblog, post, comment, moderate, photograph, and everything else along the way. My writing was not just about letters, I discovered, but images, memes, quotations, and lectures, and, and, and. If an artist can use words, I convinced myself, I'd be a writer who uses images and anything else I could.

Since 2009, *Hyperallergic* has published almost 2500 writers, and I write every day. My husband reminds me that I *do* write a lot, particularly when I feel the shame of never writing enough, and he points out there is rarely a day I don't tweet. I've come to accept that writing for me isn't only long essays, articles, or books. Sometimes it's short. Sometimes it's quick. Often it can be unexpected.

I learned that writers are not only their words but also their journeys, the words that inspire them, the record of how they got there, to whom they choose to speak, or who remembers what they've said. It can also be where they've planted ideas to step back and see them sprout.

I sometimes remind myself that Socrates never wrote anything down because he believed writing was not an effective means of communicating knowledge. When I remember that beautiful fact, and that maybe I am part of that unconventional lineage, then I tell myself, "Yes, I'm a writer, just like my grandfather was before me."

JOHN BRADY

FIGURE 17.1: John Brady. Image by Kennon Guerry.

I HAD THE worst experience writing a speech in my life after reading a book about how to write speeches. It should not have been a hard speech to write. It wasn't for a high-profile occasion, so I didn't have to fear running the gauntlet of a many-level review and the danger of death by a thousand notes. It wasn't for a special occasion like a commencement or a funeral, events that demand loftier, more memorable rhetorical flourishes and thus exert a unique pressure of their own. No, it was a straightforward policy speech. The audience was local. The policy wasn't especially grand. Every day, across the world, speechwriters sit at their desks and churn these things out by the hundreds, maybe thousands. To hear them is to forget them. Perhaps the poor cub reporter who drew the short straw and was assigned to cover the policy announcement will include a line or two from the speech and the article will actually make it onto the paper's website and the speechwriter will get to include it in their clips—if they're lucky. Otherwise, it will be gone, not consequential enough to be worth much of a memory. It was a totally routine speech, almost pure flack work.

I was blocked though. And I had only myself to blame.

* * *

Developing as a writer entails nurturing a healthy capacity for self-reflection. That's not a particularly profound insight, but a necessary one to appreciate, nonetheless. Having answers, even approximate ones, to questions ranging from *How often can I scroll through my social feeds and still make my deadline?* to *What moral commitments do I want to run through my writing?* will ease the task of not blinking under the blank page's stare.

What I know about myself is that I am particularly sensitive to an inner voice that supposedly can tell me the right way—cleverly, aesthetically, and, most importantly, socially—to write something. I will listen to that voice, and I will contort myself to conform to the voice's authoritative standard of rightness, completely made up as it may be. I will worry that I'm not listening well enough, not clearing the bar. I even know that if I don't hear it, I will be strongly tempted to seek it out and ask for its opinion.

I first heard the voice as an upperclassman in college. I had started to stretch with my writing. I tried new forms beyond the standard thesis—body with evidence—conclusion.

I experimented with different voices: humorous, ironic, morally serious. It didn't always go well. Abandoning tried-and-true methods made writing harder. And the risks I was taking wouldn't always pay off as evidenced by the negative comments and bad grades. My confidence suffered and, more and more, as I was writing, I found myself asking, "Am I doing this right?" And a voice—seemingly authoritative—started to chime in, "Nope." "Are you kidding me?" "Oh my, no!"

In 2012, as I sat at my computer, speech prep with the then mayor of Los Angeles, Antonio Villaraigosa, looming, that voice, having been bolstered by the so-called principles of good speechwriting I had recently read, was very loud and insistent. Producing each line was torture: asking that voice if it was right, determining after much consideration that it was and then, in repetitive fits of doubt, deleting all the words, rewriting them, and deleting them again as definitely not right. Even now, more than ten years later, I can feel the flop sweat coming on when I think about writing that speech. When that speech—uninspired, barely adequate—was finally done, I promised myself I would never again read advice about how to write a speech. I have kept that promise.

Rest assured, the irony that I'm now writing an essay about speechwriting is not lost on me. In my defense, this does indeed have some advice. But it's much less about the "how-to" than the "how-come" of speechwriting.

* * *

I read that book about speechwriting because of how I came to writing: from the side. I originally wanted to be a professor, not a writer. All academics write, but not all academics write well, a truth that applied to me in the early 1990s as a new graduate student at Cal Berkeley. After being told this to my face by several professors and also discovering a desire to write for audiences beyond those tolerant of mediocre, overly complex sentences, I sat down and very deliberately worked on my writing. I worked through *Style: Ten Lessons in Clarity and Grace* by Joseph M. Williams and Joseph Bizup (five stars, highly recommended). I invested in the *Little, Brown Handbook* by H. Ramsey Fowler and Jane E. Aaron and reviewed (relearned actually) the rules of grammar and syntax. Embarrassingly, this was necessary because, while I went to Catholic grade school in the late 1970s and early 1980s, I went to one infused with post-Vatican-II unorthodoxy, which meant the nuns turned us on to social justice and the evils of world hunger instead of drilling us on the seven deadly sins and the utility of diagramming sentences. And, most importantly, I got as much practical experience as I could.

As it became clear that my prospects for landing a tenure-track job were dim, owing to the fact that in the early 2000s, the market for political theorists was tight and further that the market for political theorists who specialized in post-war German political thought as applied to debates about the political participation of former Turkish guest workers was tight enough to more or less not exist, I sought out opportunities to write every time I could. It became part of my back-up plan and "diversifying my resume." I started to freelance and learned how to write for different audiences and in different styles. I learned how to write quickly. I started to get to know myself as a writer.

When I got what I consider my first full-time job as a writer—writing speeches for the mayor of Los Angeles—I admit that I was proud of the fact that I had taken an alternative route to that position, one that hadn't run through a formal credentialing process. Having spent most of the 1990s pursuing a PhD only to skid off that career track had soured me on the value of professional credentials anyway. Yet a suspicion of credentialing and pride in charting my own course didn't fully immunize me from bouts of insecurity about the quality of my work. This meant that I would be tempted to compensate for this insecurity by seeking out respected voices who could tell me how to do speechwriting right. I didn't fully understand that at the time. And so, when I read the review of that book, I ordered it and read it.

I should have trusted myself. I didn't, though. And I paid the price.

* * *

Once at a reading in Los Angeles during the second half of the aughts, the author, who also taught creative writing, was asked during the Q&A how he approached teaching. Partly in jest but also partly not, he said that on the first day of class, he had his students stand up, face the wall and shout, "Fuck the reader!" He did this to help them shrug off the inner voice of other people's expectations and, hopefully thereby, free up their creative energies.

I liked that advice: the cheekiness of it; the image of a bunch of young writers showing up expecting help with their prose and verse and instead being told to stand up and shout their heads off; the thought of the professor in the next classroom wondering what all the fuss was about. I also liked knowing that I wasn't the only one who heard voices when I wrote.

Yet the advice falls flat for speechwriting in ways that illustrate how different it can be both as writing and as a creative endeavor.

Speechwriters can't say "fuck the reader," because we don't have readers. Yes, speeches appear in print. Yes, you can buy books of speeches. Those written artifacts aren't speeches, though. Those are transcripts.

This may sound pedantic, but it's not. A speech doesn't primarily exist on the page. The speech exists in the moment it's given. In that moment, people aren't reading along. They're listening. With their ears. That's who my fellow speechwriters and I are writing for: listeners.

Every time, I "read the internet," as one of Sally Rooney's characters says, I'm reminded of the intensely visual age we live in. Phone in hand or facing a screen, I process modern life's vast information flow mostly by looking. Listening has its moments, as the earbuds that sprout from my ears and the ears of so many others indicate. Certainly, at varying times, the ear has been on more equal footing with the eye, most recently during radio's heyday. And as a once-upon-a-time political theorist, I'd be remiss to not point out that Aristotle grounds his theory of politics in humans' ability to speak (and implicitly to listen). Yet despite these and other moments, the ear has fallen far behind the eye as a portal to the human mind.

Even as I'm writing this, I see the reader scanning along. I imagine them reading for a bit and then setting the essay aside, maybe because they're tired and want to go to sleep, but more than likely because their phone just dinged. When they pick this back up, they'll re-read a few sentences to get back into it. I hope they read every word, but it's possible they'll jump around the text or skip to the conclusion and just read that. Do they linger on the sentences I constructed to please the eye? I hope that too.

Writing for the ear is different. More immediate and fleeting. As the listener is being pulled along the speech's stream, they can't go back and re-hear something that they missed or that they want to savor. So those sentences full of Russian nesting doll clauses and phrases that writers with readers will sprinkle in to demonstrate the mastery of their craft and signal their intelligence are out. The prose needs to be more direct and bite-sized even if the ideas expressed are complex and hard. It's the ear I as a speechwriter want to entice and bring joy to. Thus, the alliteration, the parallelisms, the repetition, the use of call and response, the presentation of points in threes. Used too much, they'll make a speech sound mannered. Deployed wisely though, they're little hits of aural dopamine, reminders to the listener, "Hey, this is one of the reasons why you should be paying attention!"

I love writing for the ear. I like the challenge of finding ways to be evocative and memorable within the strictures of having to be simple and direct. It's a muscular way of writing. Temperamentally, I am not a nostalgist. Nonetheless I enjoy the fact that my chosen craft has a premodern, ancient past. It's charming to have Cicero, toga and laurels included, as my profession's godfather.

Writing for the ear has also changed how I hear speeches, enriching the experience with new dimensions of feeling. Before becoming a speechwriter, when I listened to a speech, I would be in an analytical, pragmatic state of mind. I focused on the content: the policy that was being announced, the platform plank highlighted, or the person being praised. I still concentrate on those elements, but now I also tune into the something else: the craft. I'll enjoy a particularly well-phrased line. And if it's especially good, I'm not above admitting that I'll get a bit envious, wondering if I would have the chops to come up with something that effective. Admiration and envy aren't the only emotions I experience. If the speaker flubs their lines—especially if it comes at a particularly important part of the speech—I'll have nothing but sympathy for my fellow scribbler, because I know how much work can go into trying to find just the right way to express a key point. Once it is mangled or mumbled, that line's moment to shine is lost and gone forever. And for a speechwriter, that really hurts.

The second reason that speechwriters cannot pledge to stick it to their audience is that it's simply not for us to decide. The primal scream therapy that instructor ran his charges through was not only about helping them tell their inner editor to sit down and shut up. It's also a nifty encapsulation of where the locus of a fiction author's creativity lies: in having a specific voice and asserting it through their writing.

By contrast, much of a speechwriter's creativity lies in how well they renounce their own voice and take on that of another or, over the course of a career, multiple others. Of course, it's not a complete renunciation. After all, a speechwriter does make assertions and argues through the speech for points and positions. But this is done on behalf of another. And it's not a full renunciation in the sense that a speechwriter is more than just a myna bird. A central element of the job is bringing one's rhetorical and analytical skills and writer's judgment to help shape what the principal wants to express.

I leave traces in every speech. For example, I'm particularly fond of self-deprecating quips. One, because they reflect my basic sense of humor, and two, they can be an effective tool for a speaker to connect with the audience by demonstrating some humility. One such quip I'm particularly fond of and that is good for occasions when the speaker is retiring or otherwise moving on from a high-profile position is a line attributed to Eddie George, a former governor of the Bank of England. He characterized his retirement as the "transition from Who's Who to Who's He." It's a good line: short, to-the-point, easy to deliver, which is another way of saying hard to flub (see previous anecdote regarding the pain flubbing inflicts on speechwriters). It won't get a guffaw, but it will get a smile and lighten the mood in the room. But if the person I'm writing for doesn't like it or anything else in the speech, even if I know that a particular line will really land, I have to yield. Any claim I have to authorship is conditional. It's not my speech. It's not my voice.

When I tell people I write speeches, they will often ask how hard it is to write in someone else's voice. Really what they're asking is how difficult it is to pick up on the verbal preferences of the people I write for. I think this is a common understanding of what writing in someone's voice entails. It certainly is how I understood voice when I started writing. I'd look at old speeches the person I was working for had given, trying to figure out their habits and tics. I still do. Those are important ingredients of voice. It's important to know if someone is "glad to be here" or "happy to be here," whether they're thankful for the "generous" introduction or the "kind" one, and whether they like verbal signposts and throat-clearing.

Voice is more than this though, as I've come to learn. It's much richer. Like the musical voice and its various dimensions—tone, timbre, pitch—the voice of a speaker has multiple elements. It encompasses the emotional range a speaker is comfortable expressing. Voice is also about intensity. It can be bold and boisterous or moderate and mild. One of the most important components is the personal. It's crucial to know how much of their private life a person is willing to share in public and what the flavor of their sharing is. Do they share to demonstrate their vulnerability? Or do they share to show their competence? While I understand that some people want to make the wall guarding their private life tall, as a speechwriter, I appreciate working with someone who is open to a more permeable private-public barrier. I recently wrote a speech for an executive about her career history. She shared an anecdote about one of her first interviews for a corporate position and was willing to include aspects down to the color of the outfit she wore and the height of her heels. Having a storehouse of such richly detailed personal stories to drive home a speech's more abstract or complex points makes writing easier. It is also a surefire way to connect with the audience.

These and the other dimensions of voice are all opportunities for the speechwriter to demonstrate their craft. To discover the voice is to discover outlets for creativity.

Understanding a speaker's voice and delivering speeches that express it effectively and evocatively are basic professional obligations. They're something more too. They're exercises in empathy. Public speaking is hard. Survey after survey confirms its power to stoke mortal dread in mostly every human being. Giving a good speech is also very difficult. The gifted orators make it look easy. But even for them, it takes practice and work and for the merely competent, it involves even more blood, sweat, and tears. Given this, I should do everything I can to make the speaker feel comfortable and sure of themselves. One of the most significant things I can do in this regard is to make sure that the words a speaker says feel all their own.

* * *

Let me finish with some Bertold Brecht: *erst kommt das Fressen, dann kommt die Moral.* You've got to eat, and for all of the opportunities speechwriting provides for creativity and pursuit of a higher purpose, it is also a job. Not every speech, maybe in fact not a lot of them, will rise above a routine collection of talking points. I say this as someone who in the past has mined my supply of superlatives and sacrificed numerous neurons to write hosannas to jogging shoes. At the same time, I've pursued and have been fortunate to get opportunities to write for people—heads of public agencies, non-profit leaders, educators—who are working on policies or advocating for positions that I support such as increasing funding for public schools or making the criminal justice system fairer. In bringing my experiences and skills to those cases, I can align my creativity and my commitments and help amplify the political and social power of something I believe in such as the importance of civic engagement or the capacity of government to make people's lives better. That what's important. It makes the deadlines, the occasional struggles to find the right words, and speechwriting's creativity-by-proxy worth it.

JP HOWARD

FIGURE 18.1: JP Howard. Image by Nívea Castro.

A poet grows in Sugar Hill

I call myself a Black lesbian activist, writer, poet, author, curator, public interest attorney, and mama of two amazing suns (sons). All of these identities intersect and inform my writing.

My path to being an active engaged writer with my community has been circuitous at best, but this life has always been leading me toward the page, the stage, and into classrooms, writing workshops, and writers circles to celebrate the written word with my community.

I've considered myself a poet since I was in elementary school. Growing up in the 1970s in Sugar Hill, Harlem I discovered poets such as Margaret Walker, Nikki Giovanni, Langston Hughes, Lucille Clifton, and many more phenomenal Black poets uptown in Hamilton Grange Library, my local New York Public Library, blocks from the apartment I lived in with my mama. I was in elementary school when I first discovered Dudley Randall's anthology, *The Black Poets* and for me that book was a poetic bible, filled with voices of Black poets who spoke directly to me. The poets and their poems literally saved my life. As an only child being raised by a single mother, who struggled with depression, alcoholism, and who held down a government job for decades, that library and those poets' words often kept me company after school, until it was time to go home. I owe much to poet ancestors whose voices spoke to me in the Dudley anthology—Walker, Hughes, Jordan, Clifton—and to poets who still write their truths today such as Nikki Giovanni and Sonia Sanchez.

Those poets showed a skinny, painfully shy, often sad, light-skinned Black girl in pigtails in Sugar Hill, Harlem the power and magic of words. I could see the reflection of myself and hear the power of my voice when I read their poetry. When I sat at a corner table in the back of that library, reading those poems and whispering their magic words softly under my breath, after school, I lost track of time and by the time I left to go home to mama and her sadness, the sun had usually set.

My mama and I attended the storied Abyssinian Baptist Church on Lenox Avenue in Harlem and every Sunday I would recite by memory Margaret Walker's powerful and political poem "For My People" to church folks. I was about 11 or 12 years old and still painfully shy, yet Walker's words inspired me and allowed me to momentarily forget my shyness as I recited her poem. Every Sunday mama gathered a small group of womyn folk from church just to listen to me recite Walker's poem. Each week mama and those sweet womyn would clap and sing my praises, as if it was the first time they were hearing me recite that poem. From them I learned about the collective power of Black womyn to uplift and celebrate each other. Their joyful confidence in me week after week made me believe in the power of my own voice.

Poems still worked their magic on me in high school, especially after my mother took me to see a staged production of Ntozake Shange's choreopoem, *for colored girls who have considered suicide, when the rainbow is enuf*. Watching Black womyn's beautiful bodies move across that stage and speak words of resilience made me realize the magic/the power/the fierceness of Black womyn poets. Even today, when I hear contemporary Black womyn poets, including Mahogany L. Browne, t'ai freedom ford, Yolanda Wisher, Dominique Christina, Cheryl Boyce-Taylor, Staceyann M. Chin, Cynthia Manick, Pamela Sneed, and others offer their truths on the stage or the page, I feel just as inspired as I did decades ago listening to Shange's words.

I went on to college after high school and was a proud English major at Barnard College. I was the first person in my small family of womyn folk who had migrated from the deep south to go to college and with that accomplishment came great expectations that I would enter a professional field, like law or medicine. I spent those four years devouring books, including many contemporary poets. In the mid-1980s, while at Barnard, I discovered the poetry of Black, lesbian activist poets, Pat Parker, Audre Lorde, and Cheryl Clarke. While I knew it was women I was attracted to, I was still deeply in the closet back then, but hearing those womyn poets speak their truth and openly write about being Black, same-gender-loving womyn was liberating for me. Soon after, I came out of the closet to my family and friends, early in college, and in spite of clapback from my very small, Southern Christian family, I proudly remained out of the proverbial closet ever since. However, I didn't fully come out as a poet until years later.

Leaving and Coming Back Home to Poetry (the Roundabout Path)

The circuitous part of my path, away from poetry, began soon after college when I decided to go to law school to pursue public interest law. I had enjoyed volunteering for a number of local, community-centered organizations in high school and college and I wanted to give back to community after graduating from Barnard. I decided that public interest law was the right path for me at that point in my life, so I went to law school. I still loved poetry and while in law school I sometimes went to performances by local New York-based Black lesbian poets, including Cheryl Boyce-Taylor and Pamela Sneed. I would go to local Brooklyn poetry house readings with friends, often more as an observer than a participant. Time flies! I went on to become a successful public interest attorney and I did not commit myself to my passion for poetry until nearly twenty years after finishing Barnard. By then, I was in a long-term, committed relationship with my wife and we had started our sweet family.

At the age of 40, after having just given birth to our second child, I decided to pursue an MFA in creative writing at the City College of New York in the evenings. It was only then that I fully came out to the entire world as a poet. It felt liberating to finally embrace my poetry calling and arrive on the path that I had been moving toward for decades before. Not surprisingly, I focused on poetry in the MFA program and while there, I flourished, finding a supportive community of professors and fellow writers/students. Soon after, I also began applying to writing residencies and was fortunate to receive a number of prestigious residencies. I was accepted to Cave Canem's week-long writers retreat on my first attempt and went on to become a Cave Canem Graduate Fellow. While there, I studied on the campus of the University of Pittsburgh at Greensburg for annual, week-long intensive residencies for three successive summers with a world-class faculty of Black poets whose work I had read in my MFA program. I also wrote alongside fellow poets who would become lifelong friends. Next, I was selected as a Lambda Literary LGBTQ Emerging Voices Fellow in poetry. While a Lambda Fellow in Southern California for a week-long residency, I worked with the dynamic writer and instructor, Jewelle Gomez. She both inspired and encouraged me to explore difficult themes that would ultimately become part of my debut poetry collection. I was also accepted to VONA (Voices of Our Nations Arts Foundation) workshops for writers of color, and worked with the brilliant poet Willie Perdomo for a week-long residency in Berkeley, California on my first manuscript, while getting to know a wonderful cohort of writers from around the country.

My debut poetry collection, *SAY/MIRROR*, went on to become a 2016 Lambda Literary Finalist in Lesbian Poetry. That same year I was also the recipient of a Lambda Literary Foundation Judith A. Markowitz Emerging Writer Award, a tremendous honor, that acknowledged both my work in the world as a poet and my "passionate, unrelenting involvement with and on behalf of lesbians of color, all lesbians, and the LGBTQ literary community" (Lambda Literary 2016). The very next year in 2017 I was named as a Split This Rock Finalist for their Freedom Plow Award for Poetry and Activism, which acknowledged both my role as a poet and as their announcement articulated: "a non-stop force for promoting poetry by queer women of color and poets who write it." With these literary acknowledgments, I was grateful that the years I had worked toward centering myself as a poet and simultaneously supporting other poets, through my community work, was being celebrated. It was affirming to be acknowledged by a community of my peers who I respect very much. However, the road here has definitely required some serious negotiation with family and friends and ultimately lots of self-advocacy.

Advocating for Self and Bumps Along My Poetry Route

Since obtaining my MFA just over a decade ago, and pursuing my writing career head on, I have also continued to work full time as a public interest attorney this entire time, while also navigating raising two sons with my wife. I often say I am a poet who also happens to have a JD degree, but all joking aside, there have been times when it has been incredibly hard to balance parenting, my day job as an attorney, putting the work into my relationship with my wife, and making sure I nurture my own writing and get my poetry out into the world. As supportive as my wife has been, she and work colleagues and non-writer friends sometimes see me as someone who just happens to write poetry on the side. That's probably one of the most common misconceptions about writers, especially those of us who have other outside jobs that are not in the creative arts field. Folks just assume, even when they see our dedication to our craft, day in and day out, that it's just a "side" interest or hobby. Poetry and writing and my writing community are part and parcel of who I am and how I walk through the world. When folks think/say otherwise, that is hurtful.

A few years after getting my MFA, I founded a literary salon, Women Writers in Bloom Poetry Salon, which is currently in its 13th year. It has grown beyond my imagination to a monthly community space that celebrates poets, particularly marginalized women writers of color. Many of our featured authors and members are BIPOC and LGBTQIA and allies. Curating and nurturing my literary salon is a labor of literary love, and at times is like an entire other job, so I think my greatest challenges have been negotiating time to produce new work, while reminding my immediate family that I am a writer and making sure that my time to write, be involved in readings, and attend writing conferences is respected. There is definitely a lot of self-advocacy and negotiation involved in making sure my writers' needs are met. It's an ongoing process.

A Day in the Busy, But Very Full Life of This Poet

Even during this pandemic while I'm writing this, I am (still) working full time as a public interest attorney on weekdays. This past week I taught multiple writing workshops online in the evenings for community writing organizations, because I love teaching and interacting with community and the world for now has moved online, so I've adapted. My evenings are divided between running home from work to cook dinner for my family most evenings, spending down time with my wife and family, and prepping and/or teaching some of my online writing workshops. My own writing and editing usually occurs after all that, late at night when our home is quiet and most folks are sleeping. I am completing this essay at almost 2:00 a.m. for example!

Fortunately, I am, usually, but not always, a super productive night owl. I am especially grateful for my writing communities that keep me writing through much of the year. I have been part of a writing circle founded by my good friend, mentor, and phenomenal poet, Cheryl Boyce-Taylor for many years. Our writing group, Elma's Heart Circle, keeps me accountable much of the year, as we often exchange a poem a day for a number of months throughout the year. Having a community of writers to exchange work with helps to keep me consistently writing and editing, and I'm grateful for that.

Mentors and Supporters Along the Route

My wife has been my biggest, most consistent supporter. Even with the occasional clapback on my busy schedule/writing commitments, it is because of her that I've been able to take the time to accomplish my many goals as we've raised our sons. She helped keep our family together when I spent four years going to my MFA program in the evenings, while our youngest son was an infant, then toddler, while we both worked full time. She often holds our "home base" down when I travel to writing conferences and speaking engagements around the country throughout the year. While she might sometimes give me shade if I have multiple literary commitments in a row that take me away from our family, ultimately she supports me. It's been a learning process for us both, as we learn how to balance all the different aspects of our lives and support each other in our goals. My wife went on to get her masters in history in the evenings after I completed my MFA program, and I love that we are a couple that supports each other's goals to excel. During and subsequent to my MFA program, professors who mentored and supported me included Pamela Laskin and David Groff and I'm grateful to now call them both friends. I'm grateful for many poet friends who have both supported and mentored me, including fierce, queer poets, Cheryl Boyce-Taylor, Cheryl Clarke, and my friend Monica Hand, who sadly passed away a few years back. I have a large and wonderful community of poet friends who support me, who encourage me, who let me vent when I am feeling overwhelmed or being hard on myself for not making every submission deadline that I've dreamt about. They help keep me centered.

What This Literary Life Produces

I think about all that I have produced in this writer/curator/activist/community-builder life that has deeply impacted not just me, but many others whom I've come in contact with. Both my writing and my teaching consistently honor Black lesbian poet ancestors Pat Parker and Audre Lorde. This life/this ability to write my truth has been and continues to be liberating, powerful, and humbling. I almost always quote ancestor poet, Pat Parker (1978), who once said *The day all the different parts of me can come along, we would have what I would call a revolution.* I believe that with that mantra as my guide, I'm able to produce work that I am incredibly proud of. I am grateful that my poetry and my teaching style have resonated with different folks from many different backgrounds. Even during this pandemic, I have been able to connect with my poetry community month after month virtually and there is great healing in being able to bring folks together and share the power of our words. This life, this pen, these fingers, this breath has produced words that inspire and resonate and has allowed me to collaborate with my community and bring folks together from around the world to celebrate the power of our words. This life has allowed me to come out of the closet and onto the page/up onto the stage/seated in classrooms and community circles and be published in numerous anthologies, as my authentic Black lesbian activist POET self. I wouldn't change anything, not even the circuitous path that it took me to get here.

References

Parker, Pat (1978), *Movement in Black: The Collected Poetry of Pat Parker, 1961–1978*, Ithaca, N.Y.: Firebrand Books.

Split This Rock (2017), "Freedom Plow Award for Poetry & Activism 2017 – Recipient, Finalists, and Honorable Mentions," https://www.splitthisrock.org/programs/freedom-plow-award-for-poetry-activism/2017-freedom-plow-award-for-poetry-activism/. Accessed September 18, 2024.

Valenzuela, Tony, (2016), "Bryan Borland and JP Howard Named Lambda Literary's Judith A. Markowitz Emerging Writer Award Winners," Lambda Literary, May 3, https://lambdaliterary.org/2016/05/bryan-borland-and-jp-howard-named-lambda-literarys-judith-a-markowitz-emerging-writer-award-winners/. Accessed September 18, 2024.

KAREN TABORN

FIGURE 19.1: Karen Taborn. Image by David Flores.

MY JOURNEY TO become a published writer was a long road with many curves and challenges along the way. I grew up in a family deeply engaged in racial justice and Black empowerment activism. My father was a maverick Black home builder in Cleveland, Ohio during the 1950s. Dad was following in the footsteps of his grandfather and his namesake, Albert White who made a reputation as a leading mason who built the founding buildings of Kalamazoo, Michigan's Western Michigan University (see Flynn 2024). Two generations later, my father's dad's company, Taborn Realty, built hundreds of affordable homes for first-time, Black homeowners encountering redlining. My mother also came from a family engaged in racial activism. Mom's great grandfather served in the Civil War with the US Colored Troops and her grandfather was a noted journalist in the Black historical press. Mom carried the tradition of activism forward too. For a few years she was the vice president of our local NAACP chapter in Kalamazoo, Michigan and later in her life she led educational "Healing Racism" workshops with members of her religion, the Baha'i Faith.

Despite my family background of activism, while I was young I experienced anti-Black sentiments and actions in my social milieu that left me bewildered about race in America and my place in the country's racial-social structure. In the predominately White, Midwestern communities where I grew up, I encountered schoolmates and teachers who expressed demeaning assumptions of what it was to be Black.

One experience took place in grade school, around 1965–66. For some unknown reason, my teacher posed an inappropriate question to her young students. "Who can tell us what Hell is?" she asked! A young classmate raised his hand and blurted out "It's where colored people go when they die!" I was the only student of color in the class and I can still remember the entire classroom of fifth graders turning, seemingly in slow motion, to fix their glares upon me! I shrunk into my seat, wanting to become invisible. The experience led me to strategically alter my classroom demeanor thereafter. I adopted a performative comportment that was harmless, girlish, and non-threatening. I began to imitate the performance of the then popular, female, bimbo TV star Goldie Hawn. It was the only strategy I could conceive in my young mind to remove myself from the stigma of race! Although this was my initial experience with racism, it was by no means the last. My family experienced many racist encounters in my youth, including being assaulted by a sinister, midnight, cross burning in our yard! In the years following my middle school experience, I became familiar with racism in America and I learned that my and my family's experiences with racism were not exceptional for Black Americans. Our experiences were part of normative American social structure.

Nevertheless, because my family was middle class I experienced alienation from the few Black students in my schools too. The majority of my Black schoolmates emerged from the north side of town, a struggling ghetto, while my family lived in neighboring White middle class areas. We attended my father's liberal, predominately White, Unitarian Church. Also, we were not recent immigrants from the South; thus, we didn't speak with a southern accent as my Black schoolmates did. We stood out from my Black schoolmates who envisioned us as being a pseudo Black-White family and there was often tension and resentment from our Black school peers expressed toward me and my siblings.

By my teenage years, I had been profoundly affected by hierarchical conceptions and representations of race stemming from mainstream, i.e., White society, that placed Black people and Blackness at the bottom of the social structure. It seemed that everywhere I looked, from advertisements in print and television media, to children's books and adult novels, to news reports, music, and music-making, there were subtle and not-too-subtle suggestions equating Black American people to being uncivilized and uncouth. Contrarily, conceptions and representations of western European and White American culture were equated to being civilized, cultivated, and refined. This racialized social mountain seemed insurmountable to me and I was perplexed with how to confront the dilemma.

Then, one summer, my parents sent me to live with family members in another section of the country. It was the 1970s and the band Earth, Wind and Fire (EWF) was producing the hottest music pumping through the US airwaves. My cousins were constantly playing EWF's music throughout their home. I had of course heard EWF's music prior to my visit but I had rejected the band. At the time, I was a burgeoning musician myself and I followed the music of the popular, mostly White, folk-rock musicians of the era such as Joni Mitchell, James Taylor, and

Laura Nyro. EWF performed in outlandish costumes, reflecting a distant African or Egyptian past that seemed odd to me at best.

I believe now that I had unconsciously absorbed some of the racist ideology surrounding me and that this influenced my inability to see and hear EWF's message of universal peace and love. But while listening to the band's music, far from my familiar home surroundings, in what I now understand to be a "liminal space," I heard the band anew. For the first time, I heard the band's spiritual message in their lyrics and in their performance. Through this renewed experiential encounter with EWF, I began to question my preference for predominantly White folk-rock music and musicians and my tendency to hold Black music in general, in suspicion. I knew that somehow my perception had been racialized and from that moment on I made a personal commitment to question and examine the socialization of race in my own mind and in US society more deeply.

A few years later, my liminal experience with EWF was followed by a similar "awakening" while listening to the jazz, maverick musician, John Coltrane. By 1975, at the age of 19, I was committed to becoming a jazz singer and musician myself. For me, jazz was not only based on my love for the music. I also found solace in the jazz community, set apart from mainstream White society in our mutual love for Black musical excellence.

When I began college, a few years later, at the age of 21, I continued studying jazz history and performance as a singer and a pianist. I became a jazz vocal major, eventually moving to New York City in 1983 where I studied with jazz singers Abbey Lincoln and Sheila Jordan and jazz history with the renowned bassist, Ron Carter. I continued along this trajectory earning a master's degree in jazz vocal education in 1988 from NYU.

It was only after receiving my Master of Arts in jazz that I stumbled upon an opportunity to write about Black history. In 1992, a consortium of New York professionals working on a project called the Strivers Center Project—to revitalize 135th Street in Harlem—invited me to conduct secondary research on Harlem's rich Black history. I was longing for this opportunity! I dived in with complete abandon, reading every book on the subject that I could get my hands on. I knew that this opportunity could possibly open doors for me beyond being a singer and musician, to become an historian and a writer, something I privately long for. I produced a paper titled "What Made Harlem Famous" and the finalized Strivers Center Project resulted in a Harlem Walk of Fame, installed on West 135th Street between Seventh and Eighth Avenues.

My paper was influential in helping me acquire my first adjunct teaching position in the humanities department at the New School for Social Research where I taught Harlem history from 1993 to 1995. I concluded each class by taking my students on a tour of Harlem.

Following this experience, I was invited to teach another course of my choice at the New School. The country was experiencing racial turmoil following the Los Angeles police beating of Rodney King and the subsequent exoneration of the officers involved. I found myself deeply emotionally engaged in these developments and I proposed teaching a course over the next five years, titled "Race and Sex in American Life." I developed the curriculum for this course using the biographical and theoretical texts of Black women writers such as Audre Lorde, bell hooks, Maya Angelou, and others. Far beyond an academic course, the class turned into a profound analytical reading, a personal experience of sharing and deep listening, and critical thinking for everyone involved. After teaching this course, I returned to focusing on singing and playing piano, pursuing vocal performance engagements in New York City.

In 2000, I decided to return to school to pursue a second MA degree in ethnomusicology at Hunter College. I was profoundly interested in socio-cultural developments and ethnomusicology provided me with the tools to examine such phenomena. I was taught an interdisciplinary research/study approach, using theoretical, experiential, musical, and historical studies to follow my interests. While my area of research was not on an African American subject, I gained immeasurable knowledge and experience in conducting first person interviews, doing archival research, and examining theoretical hypotheses to do critical thinking analysis. I and my colleagues in the program viewed our professor, Barbara Hampton, as a brilliant Black woman and (after initial doubts) she became deeply committed to the success of my project.

After successfully completing my MA in ethnomusicology, I completed four years of ethnomusicology doctoral coursework at Indiana University in Bloomington. However, I switched the focus of my study after my second year and after not receiving the support I needed from my advisors to complete the PhD, I decided to end my doctoral studies before completion of my degree.

Returning to New York City in 2010, I was hired to teach a course on understanding cultural diversity as an adjunct professor at York College in Jamaica, Queens. The course was an undergraduate requirement with sections taught by a number of professors at the college. However, following 2015, it was downsized for financial considerations. Unfortunately, as the last professor to be hired, my position at the school was suddenly in jeopardy and my tenure came to an end.

Following this, I found myself wondering what to do next and I decided to return to my research and writing on Harlem. I had always wanted to expand my paper, "What Made Harlem Famous" to include more in-depth information on influential Harlem individuals and movements during the era of the Harlem Renaissance. I also wanted to do archival research on photographs and/or take photographs myself and I wanted to develop tour routes toward the publication of a full-fledged book. By 2016, I had a manuscript ready to send out to publishing companies. I submitted several book proposals to publishers and was signed by Rutgers University Press in the fall of the same year.

The publication of my book, *Walking Harlem: The Ultimate Guide to the Cultural Capital of Black America* (2018) focuses on multiple socio-cultural-artistic-political developments of a primary historically Black American community. I focus on the visual, literary, and (of course) the musical arts, and socio-cultural and political movements that make Harlem an internationally renowned community. My background in ethnomusicology was significant in providing me with archival research skills and in tying together contextual developments gleaned from autobiographies, biographies, historical press articles, record liner notes, and texts that examine art, literary, cultural, and political developments.

Upon the release of *Walking Harlem*, I began offering tours of Harlem to the public. Beyond historical data offered in typical commercial tours, I include stories of incidents, events, and experiences of what happened where, why, and with whom to awaken tourists' imaginations and create an experiential connection to Harlem's iconic Black history and culture.

KATHY ENGEL

FIGURE 20.1: Kathy Engel. Image by Philippe Cheng.

MY PARENTS SPLIT in 1959, when I was 4 (I think that's when). We lived in Manhattan. Two years later my sister, brother, and I moved with my mom—who married a potato farmer—to eastern Long Island, near the sea and potato and corn fields. My dad remained in Manhattan. When I would visit him on alternate weekends, at night in my pullout bed in his Upper West Side living room, he would read poems he loved to me at night: William Butler Yeats, John Donne, Gerard Manley Hopkins, and parts of the Old Testament. He wasn't religious but loved the book as beautiful literature. Our favorite was the Book of Ruth, something about the loyalty and love between Ruth and Naomi. I didn't understand the poems, but I loved the music, and that he loved them and shared that with me. He also read me *Winnie the Pooh*. I self-identified as Eeyore at a fairly young age!

At some point, we started playing this game of leaving limericks around for each other, always ending with the teasing refrain: *I got you last*! We'd leave them attached to the lamp chain, in a pot, inside a sweater. Maybe that early recognition of the drive to have the last word meant something important about writing—to have the last word!

My dad took me for piano lessons when I was eight or nine. I was terrible, didn't practice enough, and couldn't quite get the notes. So, the piano teacher suggested I write stories to the music. That freed me. I wrote "The Scream that Never Stopped," "Avery the Cat," and who knows what else.

When I was 10 or 11, in the small, home-grown school my mother and other parents started, I had a teacher who encouraged my writing. He took us with notebook and pen to fields of rye, to the beach on windy days, honored my unedited lines. I wrote about divorce, the train between mother and father, sea and cement, horses and protests. I wrote about wilting pumpkins in a field, the solace of cutting wind, salt air, and early adolescent melancholia. My mom sensed that I would connect to the poems of Anne Sexton and gave me *To Bedlam and Part Way Back*. I was hooked. I read the poems over and over and over sucked into the emotional intensity and music. The poems invited me to dwell in an emotional and linguistic landscape, an embodied intensity for which I yearned.

Meanwhile, after becoming a teenager, my brother moved to the city to live with our dad and go to school there. Around 1967, he joined a writing group in Harlem called "What's Happening," for which June Jordan and Terry Bush were mentors. I couldn't have known that years later I would become close to June, that she would become a powerful teacher (although not officially) and a friend and sister in political struggle and cultural work. At that time, my brother also met and introduced me to the work of Victor Hernández Cruz with whom the group was connected.

I never stopped writing, but somehow by the time I got to college I thought I needed to restrain my voice, push out the "I." I didn't know anything about form and although I knew discipline and practice in physical activities, I didn't know it in writing and was even afraid of it. My first writing class as an undergraduate at Sarah Lawrence College in the fall of 1973 came as a shock. It was a fiction workshop with Cynthia Macdonald. I was clueless about the structure of a story. She didn't hold back with her critique. I was stunned to learn that to make something good, I couldn't simply write free flow. I went on to work with poets Jane Cooper, Jean Valentine, and Galway Kinnell. I was not, by a long shot, one of the strongest in the group of student poets at the time. This came as a rude awakening.

I think poetry was always for me a way of being and sensing the world as much as writing it. Rhythms, moods, objects, animal life, loss, birth all made lyrical sense to me even if not rational sense. Measurements, categories, and what seemed to be arbitrary separations between almost anything seemed imposed, unnatural, and counter poetic. I can't explain it.

I worked at the Academy of American Poets after graduating, surrounded by amazing writers who participated in our programs and schooled by the brilliant, eccentric, and visionary Elizabeth Kray. In 1979 I think it was, I went with my father and my partner, artist Jonathan Snow, to Seabrook, New Hampshire to join our friend, the writer Grace Paley, and great numbers of people in what was called an anti-nuclear "occupation." It was there I met the poet Denise Levertov with whom I had corresponded as part of my job at the academy. This time she was sitting in a dusty circle on the ground reading poems to other "occupiers." I felt I was home. Denise and I agreed later we were actually meant to meet that way.

Soon after Seabrook, I left the Academy in 1979 and became a full-time organizer with the New York Mobilization for Survival. My life became a seesaw between intensive, burnout political organizing and brief breaks at the MacDowell Colony, or the

Blue Mountain Center, or my childhood home, for euphoric exhale, nature, and writing.

I hid behind the political work. What I had to negotiate and bear and grind through was the fear of not being good enough at what was most truly and powerfully me, and the sense of affirmation I got from offering myself to the world, even as I became more and more unbalanced. I worked with many others to blend those pulls and passions, insisting always that without the integral engagement of art, imagination, and cultural work, no real social change would happen. Our cultural work insisted on integrating on every level, the imaginative and artistic, with strategic organizing for justice, equity, and peace. Still, the artists' contribution was often viewed in my experience as the dessert, not the dinner, an extra or add-on, rather than essential to every aspect of imagining and creating a more equitable, sustainable, joyful, loving world.

I became obsessed with the notion of language as transformation, not for, but *as*. It was June Jordan who taught me how to read the newspaper to understand power and differentiate between active and passive verbs in articles and headlines, between who is blamed and when something "just happens," according to race, gender, class, age, location. Any separation between art and politics, imagining and organizing, from that point on never made sense to me.

In the early 1980s, through my cultural organizing, I met, worked with, and in many cases became friends with a world of writers and artists, and cultural workers from around the world, who became my artistic community, my light and oxygen. These brave, brilliant artists showed me the possible and also the legacy that brought us to our work. They mentored me, perhaps sometimes without realizing it. They uplifted, inspired, and helped me feel less alone.

Although I never stopped writing, I continued to put my own work second to the collaborative, community-driven work, and I fell into the role of being a bridge between artists and organizers. I didn't give poetry (or myself) what was called for to be fully inside my craft, to be whole in my potential power. I largely denied my yearning for quiet, for spirit life, for nature. I have to admit it was fear that held me back.

The ride toward a different balance has been and continues to be marvelous, scary, and confusing. Yet today I allow myself to honor the yearning for quiet, for digging deep for the reveal that a poem, any writing or making, might be.[1]

As I continue to live, I am leaning toward a day to day that will be more grounded in writing and making, listening, and even waiting. I'm not good at waiting but I'm teaching myself. I did think of much of my political work as a form of poetic engagement at the time (the international women's human rights organization MADRE, I cofounded with a group of women and led from 1983 to 1989, for example, or the work with the Women in Prison Project in the 1990s, and more). Now I long for the space to wander, linger inside and around with language and what comes before language, with it, beyond it, to trust the necessity for slow and deep introspection to create. That's where I'm headed!

Today I write a haiku every morning, thanks to the example and invitation of my beloved sister and mentor Sonia Sanchez. I write more intensively when the academic semester is over and in April, when I'm blessed to write a poem each day with a wonderful group of women poets, Elma's Heart Circle, convened by poet Cheryl Boyce-Taylor. They keep me going. My best friend Alexis De Veaux does. My daughters do. I thank my mother who says she doesn't always get poetry but has always encouraged me to be brave. My partner who loves poetry and listens to early drafts with a keen ear, does. Ocean, trees, deer, birds, fields, do. And those called students, with whom I co-learn, uplift and inspire me. I am looking toward living in writing which means also living in not always writing, not always doing, in the fullness, the quiet, the uncertainty, the listening, to put words to the seeming impossible and dangerous—daring to open, to not know, to excavate and embrace, to relearn each day. Now I trust in the tiniest of blooms, the intimate.

No matter what happens with a work, what sustains me is the making of it, fidelity to that process, connection with poets, community, memory, deep attention, living, embodied archives, from the earliest times to the unknown memory of the future. I'm drawn more deeply each day to the natural world, the spirit world, the most intimate touch, our uni- no, multiversal thread—through the lines, the listening, the song, the cracks, the liminal space between. I dwell on the practice of *Re vision* as Adrienne Rich translated *revision*. I call this practice love: to love enough, to honor enough to speak what must be spoken, to write what insists on being written, to savor even the most terrifying memory, thought, experience, to work in and through the wholeness and complicatedness of being. We change a word, make more space, notice, take notice. We risk being misunderstood. My challenge is to say and write the thing that is most scary—and most beautiful in its reveal.

Note

1. This is a nod to artist Valerie Maynard who said to my friend, the writer Alexis De Veaux: "You cannot write what hasn't been revealed, Alexis."

Reference

Flynn, Erin (2024), "Black Mason Broke Barriers, Laid First Building Blocks for Learning at Western," *WMU News*, February 8, https://wmich.edu/news/2024/02/74599. Accessed 28 June 2024.

KEALEY BOYD

FIGURE 21.1: Kealey Boyd. Image by Rebecca Caridad.

ON A BRIGHT October afternoon, I met the Japanese artist Shimabuku for an article about his video "Do Snow Monkeys Remember Snow." He arrived directly to our interview from Okinawa in a jet-lagged daze. A brief walk from the Denver Art Museum lobby to his installation was punctuated with many stops by the works of other artists. Sometimes he mumbled questions or proclaimed to know the maker, but mostly we stared together. He rattled off this feedback to the museum press person named Jenna when we arrived at his space: "This room is too dark"; and "these pamphlets are nice. Can I have a bunch?" Once settled, I asked, "So, why was it important to test if snow monkeys remember snow?" He answered, "Maybe it is not important."

When art critics speak eloquently and admirably of our profession, I wonder if we actually are in the same field. I remember hearing writer Jessica Lynne on a panel describe the genre of criticism as art and I choked on my own saliva. Her assertion is radical. Sometimes it feels like I am making strides in the field, a true contributor and comrade. Usually, it feels like I'm launching content from a speeding car window, hardly anyone pausing to consider what is at stake, let alone read it. It has been four years since my first major publication of art criticism and I am in my second year writing full time. It means I have been writing long enough to know how little I know and to become uncomfortable with the routes available to publish my work. On top of that I'm 40. I know Twitter shouts the names of creative women who got their start late in life, after their kids were grown, but it's always the same five names. Besides, my kids won't be grown for another ten years. Isn't that when the UN predicts we will all be baked potatoes?

I arrived at writing out of frustration. The allure of my career on Wall Street after eight years was fading in early 2008. During that year, people I initially respected seemed to pull off masks to reveal that they were actually assholes. I began plotting an exit that would set in motion a profession in art history that I wanted since college but couldn't then afford to explore. After 12-hour days as a structured products saleswoman on a Credit Suisse trading floor, I would attend night classes at NYU, reach out to old professors and study for the GRE. About half of my graduate school applications were in their manila envelopes when the market collapsed, Lehman closed, people lost their homes, and both my husband and I lost our jobs. I was accepted to graduate school at the University of Chicago a few months later. When I completed my art history training, I joined my husband in Denver where he had found a new job in the financial industry.

The cultural terrain was spirited, but uneven and the art writing was exclusive to two men in the city. Instead of throwing stones at their contributions, I decided to toss in my hat. A national platform, *Hyperallergic*, bit on my first ever pitch, but I was the one who was hooked.

There is tremendous satisfaction in observing and documenting the delicacies of art making. When I witness an artist ascend from some small venue in the foothills of Colorado to a grand stage, I become emotional. Maybe I am a cog in the art market's capitalist machine, but thousands of eyes can shift to a body of work because someone wrote a compelling or dissenting view, and that ripple can grow into a tidal wave seen from the coasts.

Selfishly, I write because I love research, the hunt for great ideas, and the validation publication brings to both.

Doubt is my shadow in this journey. It clings to my heels, a specter of rejection. Last year, I had an incredible year publishing 35 articles and speaking at several public events. This year I focused on contributing to more books, longer essays—more experimenting, less rapid rounds of publishing. The result was more rejection. Several months would pass with only bad news in my inbox. No explanation, just "no," or worse, silence. No matter how much Instagram Oprah says failure is shaping my future, I see it as a fickle teacher at best. It is not good, it is not moral, it just exists. Of course, it prompts self-reflection, but mostly it just jams up my day. If doubt holds me in place, time runs. How should I structure my time? A residency? Book research? Reading? Writing? Do I pitch that idea again or move on? Was this rejection due to the angle or clarity of language … maybe both. Rework it? Nah, there is not enough time. I switched careers to writing very late in life and often wonder if it is made for a younger heart. I convince myself my experience serves me better than youth. Maybe.

The day is long. My two young sons rise early (it seems even earlier if I try to write before 6 a.m.). After I get them ready for school, I teach art history courses as an adjunct at a local university, research a pitch or article, visit studios and exhibitions, and keep a crowded calendar of coffee dates with new colleagues. Jerry Saltz said it was impossible to be a critic in a small town, which is true, but not for the reason he suspects. Maintaining the infrastructure of a writing career is its own full-time gig. A sloppy or cruel critic can survive in a small city, but they cannot expand their reach.

Writing is a bizarre profession and I spent nearly a decade taking Wall Street clients—grown men—to strip clubs and Medieval Times. That was all after a day of enduring name calling as one of only five women on a crowded trading floor. ("Parrot" bothered me the most.) The common ground between writing and finance is that both careers are isolating. On Wall Street, I had to act as if I was the smartest person in the room, could out drink every man at the bar, be likable, be a rockstar. But I could never say "I don't understand this product," or "I don't know why the market moved." I could never pull back the curtain to show the human running the machine. In writing, readers want the curtain gone. They want vulnerability, transparency, and struggle, but they also want to see success. Once a triumph is captured, the reward is a medallion inscribed with "what else?" Writing is an unromantic and brutally solitary exercise. No one is waiting for anything to happen. If I took some other job and never wrote again, I suspect few people would notice. Twitter would barrel forward. An intern would copy the talking points of a press release and many artists would be satisfied to have their name in print even if the language describing their work repeats the obvious.

The isolation may explain why I sacrifice my time to say "yes": yes to that critique two hours away; yes to moderating your mom-in-the-arts panel; yes to that fundraiser for your book. The daily negotiation of how to utilize time is a mental trap that can be eased by mentors especially when the expectation is that a good idea will always land somewhere even though it seldom does. Stephanie Su and I met in graduate school as students in 2009. We talk frequently about our work and our kids—in that order. My admiration for her writing discipline and intense focus on the parts of her career within her control has never faded. Her critiques such as "I see people liked this article, but I wonder what problems you resolve?" are doled out with a kindness and neutrality that feels like we are editing a third person in the room. I enjoy the challenge of writing in a way that appeals to her, an academic, and still lands with a reader on their commute. Maybe doing both is a fool's errand, but if it were, she would probably tell me.

My professional practice has been uniquely shaped by Hrag Vartanian. He encouraged me to increase the amount of content I published and to submit ideas more diligently. His advice sharpened my voice and vantage point on what readers and editors want. It was the best crash course in writing.

My family is another uncomfortable mentor and critic of my work. This year my 8-year-old son was diagnosed with dyslexia. It is a cruel thing, altering how words sound and challenging his retrieval of known words. He doesn't see words backwards as many people understand the disability, but each time he sees a word he must decode it like it is the first time. He finds refuge in the visual, through drawing and building. He joyfully joins many of my site visits and it is in his exuberance for the creative world that we find each other. My 6-year-old son protests each gallery and museum visit, often sitting in the middle of the sidewalk until I yield to his will. He cannot be coerced to care.

Writing can feel like a version of dyslexia, causing me to hear only the negative or false sincerity. Flipping words for the aesthetics of flow, second guessing an angle or a transition—it seems to come so effortlessly to everyone else. Is it this laborious for my reader? Will they bail on my story, never to be won back?

Convincing someone that art is worthwhile for its own sake is perennially the strategy of artists and writers, but it's a bad one. I think of the boy refusing to enter the gallery, unwilling to join any part of the conversation while passively participating in culture when he demands "Old Town Road" on the stereo or reads a Marvel comic book at bedtime.

I consume every article about the death of the critic. They feel familiar. When applying to finance jobs in college, people constantly said that computers were replacing traders, as if the only trader was the kind on the NY Stock Exchange, providing a stage set for CNBC's Squawk Box. Hundreds of traders work in each New York City bank, managing the risks of their firm. I never was a trader, but I worked with them closely. They are grumpy human databases that know prices, volumes, and client behavior, all of which would sputter out in a mix of curse words and pregnant pauses meant to make one uncomfortable enough to walk away.

The critic today is savvy, migratory, harder to point out and say "there." Just glance at writer bylines. They are a laundry list of symbolically valuable jobs each taking equal priority: curator, writer, artist, place maker. Today's artwork requires more research and competency of history, theory, identity, replacing the shoot-from-the-hip strategy of previous prototypes. In that motley mix is the critic as influencer, selling Moncler on Instagram or a vacation spot near Marfa. Who would contest the exchange of symbolic value for a monetary one? How else are critics supposed to make a living and save for the future when our careers are being replaced by Buzzfeed quizzes?

As a critic in "the middle" I am in strange company compared to those on the coasts. Perhaps that is why the critic's conundrum feels weary. To see art, I drive six hours to Santa Fe, where the light is lavender like a Blumenschein painting, or two hours to Wyoming over a mountain pass only populated by elk. I navigate on foot through a motorcycle convention on my way to an Anne Brigman show in Reno. I perpetually feel like I'm living among people who history will remember too late and I must record them. Is there a finder's fee for that? I equally worry I'm in the monkey house at the zoo, wondering if my surroundings stink and I stopped smelling it. The latter idea makes me paranoid that I'm out of sync with important trends, pressing all research past the needs of the pitch, devouring more time.

Ironically, in the personal essay of an art critic there is no big thesis to prove or resolution claimed. I remain where I started, choking on the hidden challenges of a life I chose. It feels unnatural to annotate the burdens of this profession because it is a privilege to write and have my voice heard. It is also peculiar to wager on the empty page, but that is where I search for myself, and to my own surprise, return each day.

KHADIJA GODING

FIGURE 22.1: Khadija Goding. Image by K. Goding.

WHEN I THINK about how I discovered my calling as a writer, I have to credit how I came into this world. My story begins in January of 1982, during a blizzard that had swept my soon-to-be-corner-of-the-planet, Brooklyn, New York. My very pregnant, 31-year-old mother was snacking on Lays potato chips and watching *The Jeffersons* when her water broke. In preparation for my arrival, she had taken a break from completing her graduate degree in early childhood education, primarily because her last trimester was chock full of projectile vomiting and back aches.

My father, a freelance photographer and construction worker, was at a work site in the Bronx when he received the call. My father's elaborate version of that day involves his boss relaying the message about my impending arrival, followed by his leaping almost 10 feet off scaffolding, hopping on his bike, and riding all the way to Downstate Medical Center to meet my mother. My parents, two loving people in temporary denial of their incompatibility, had married four years prior. And here I came, ready to greet the world, the daughter of two Brooklyn baby boomers; my mother's one and only child, my father's fourth.

I view my birth story, in all its versions—with varying recollections of exactly how cold it was that day and how many blankets my grandmother wrapped me in to take me home—as the first introduction to myself. The story is full of love, and each time my mother told it, she made sure to add that it was the happiest day of her life. By my third birthday, my parents had separated. This story memory became the glue that held my beginnings together, amidst the ebb and flow of divorce and the shift to only seeing my dad on alternating weekends.

I was about two and a half years old when I started writing during the summer of 1984. When I say this, people usually look at me like I am crazy. But in all truth, I carried out my mother's ambitions without hesitation. Writing small words, coupled with attempts at drawing people and our giant, moody tabby named Nguyen, became an obsession. Mom was a kindergarten teacher, and a talented illustrator, so by default, our entire apartment was labeled with colorful index cards. In fact, by the time I could sit up on my own, mom was teaching me how to express myself verbally and on paper. Every day she would guide my tiny right hand with a crayon, repeating the sounds of every letter we drew, slowly and patiently. I must have been around 18 months when she awoke to discover that I had finally attempted my name in all caps, K-H-A-D-I-J-A, in bold, red, indelible marker across the living room wall.

As time went on, my father would pick me up on the weekends for our habitual museum visits. The Metropolitan Museum of Art was my favorite. Over lunch, he would break out a pencil and paper and ask me to write something about our day together. "What did you enjoy today?" and "How do you feel?" he would ask. I would excitedly answer, erasing and rewriting until my small hands formed a perfect alignment of words.

I loved recapping my days. When dad found himself split between his new family, work, and time, I would write him letters, to catch him up on all that he was missing. By kindergarten, I was writing to several people, sending unsolicited accounts of what I had for breakfast and how I dressed myself for the first time, among other exciting milestones.

Blame it on growing up as an only child, but correspondence in the form of snail mail meant everything to me. Maybe it was the realization that people listened better when they read my words, rather than trying to listen to a verbally super-inquisitive child. At the time, the audible world seemed so inundated with distractions ... like Oprah and Donohue, work, bills, phone calls, and all the adult things that made my parents often slightly out of reach. Letter writing became my fishing rod, the envelope the bait, and the letter the hook.

My elementary school years, 1988–93, were defined by repeated trips to the library and spending hours at Barnes and Nobles. I lived for literature. Information was my life source. When Scholastic started issuing our school with weekly newsletters on Tuesdays, it may as well have been Christmas morning for me. I read that paper from cover to cover, and I vowed that one day I would make a newsletter of my own.

When I had reached the second grade in September 1990, my mom had gifted me my first diary. It was and still may be the greatest gift I have ever received. That small pink book was my introduction to consistently chronicling my emotions, the events that shaped me, and logging those I liked and those I wanted sent to Mars. That tiny pink book kicked off eleven straight years of journaling and solidified that writing, for me, was as intrinsic as breathing.

My diary also became the inspiration for entering literary competitions in school, by the time I graduated the fifth grade. By summer of 1993, I had won several poetry awards and earned publication in two child anthologies. I was on my way. There was nothing else but writing in my frontal lobe. I was inspired, and I carried the encouraging words of my teacher, Mrs. Miller, deep in my chest. "Khadija, I can't wait to read your books when you get older," she would say. I would walk away, beaming.

By high school, I started writing for the school newspaper and quickly became editor in chief. The year was 1996, and it was the first time I found my creativity stifled by the confines of a Catholic high school administration. It was frustrating, and occasionally I published things without approval, which resulted in academic threats and racist criticism.

Growing up, I had seen reporters like Sue Simmons and watched *Like It Is* with my mom like clockwork. Representation mattered in my household. My mother saw to that. I was inspired to have my own roundtable discussions, asking family members to endure my obsessions for topics ranging from the implications of scientists cloning sheep, to President Clinton's impeachment. I started seeking out role models, Black and Brown women who I felt shared in my experiences. I fell in love with journalists like Lisa Ling and Linda Villarosa. Their very existence confirmed my own. I wanted to shake things up too and engage with people from all walks of life. The summer of 1998 I actually mustered up the courage to send Ms. Villarosa a letter informing her of how much her work meant to me. As luck would have it, she responded. Her letter was full of words of encouragement and kindness. It was the best letter I had ever received, shaping my next steps in determining how to handle the growing pains of young adulthood.

My teenage years were full of contradictions. I was a skinny, tall, and awkward nerd with big aspirations, but totally clueless on where to fit in. Hormones, first time attractions, peer pressure, and battles with self-acceptance led me to feel like an alien in my own skin. I felt happiest when I was learning and exploring new spaces. I looked forward to every summer when my mother and I would take our annual vacation to a state or country that was new to us. I wrote about every journey and jotted down notes about every single person that I met, along with their contact information and picture. I gained pen pals, from South Africa to London and beyond, many of which I am still friends with today. Connectivity was my middle name. I was inspired by the variety of souls that life happened to conjure.

Summer of 1997, I was feeling particularly frustrated with my life. My mom and I had gotten into an argument, so I decided to hop on the A train to the East Village to peruse CDs at Kim's Underground. I loved that store, and that particular day, it happened to have a display of compact discs labeled "Riot Girl." I had never heard of the genre, but to satisfy my curiosity I picked up a copy of Bikini Kill's *Revolution Girl Style Now*, which was originally released in 1991. I walked over to Washington Square Park, popped the CD in my Walkman and sat down by the water fountain to take a listen. Within seconds my mind was blown. I had dabbled in punk rock, and sang in a band from time to time, but I had never heard an all-female rock group shouting down the patriarchy.

That album catapulted me into the riot girl movement, a world of young feminist punk rock expression (albeit a little too monochromatic) and led me to the greatest discovery at the time, an associated literary world of small DIY magazines called "zines," made for and by alternative punk youth across the nation.

Within the year, I started writing one of my own. I named it *Publik*, adding the letter k for the first letter of my name. I feverishly chronicled my personal truths, writing and collaging about music, identity, peer pressure, and fitting in (or the lack thereof). I was so excited to be a part of this world that I started doing my high school homework in the wee hours of the morning, just so I could rush home after school to make my zine. On the weekends, I spent long days at Kinko's Office and Print Services photocopying hundreds of pages and stapling my zine into existence. It was my little clandestine operation. These were the most honest literary years of my life.

At the age of 19, my zine writing came to a screeching halt when I was diagnosed with lupus. I was a sophomore at Barnard College, grappling with kidney disease and sheer uncertainty. I wanted to write, but my thoughts were jumbled. I wanted straight "A's," but my body needed rest. I spent my days between school and hospital visits, trying to make sense of my own trajectory. I was blocked and traumatized. Healing and graduating college was the only silver lining, and over the next few years I endured a slow but steady victory.

It would take another five years before I found myself writing again, and this time it was for my very first job. After college graduation in May 2005, I went traipsing around Europe looking for creative writing internships. After hitting quite a few dead ends, a friend of mine back home sent me a job listing for a major financial news and analytics company. They hired me on the spot, that same year in October.

Catapulted into the professional world of financial journalism and analytics, I embarked on a huge departure from all that I knew. My previous internship at Chase bank, a caveat to receiving a full college scholarship, had gotten me through the door. The job was a major sacrifice of insanely long hours, stressful data analysis, micromanagement, and patriarchal power trips, in exchange for the excellent healthcare that my parents urged me not to pass up. I also had the opportunity to travel the world with a diverse group of young, twenty-something writers.

The experience was fun. For the first time I was making money—good money. For eight solid years, from 2005 to 2013, I welcomed the distraction from the type of social journalism I had desired. And then, as life would have it, I was hit with another heavy challenge. My kidneys failed. One September afternoon in 2006, while I was vacationing in Paris, my kidneys conspired to shake things up. I rushed home, went straight to the hospital, and learned of my fate. Once again, I stopped writing.

In the interim years I received a successful kidney transplant—praise be to my incredible mother—and enjoyed a quiet period of recovery. In January 2013, I eased back into "normalcy" with a part-time job at a Brooklyn arts organization, and took on creative freelance opportunities. I also, by chance, stumbled into the world of voice over acting. It took a total of three years until I was ready to fully return to my calling. But, this time, I did it without fear, irrational bosses, and the stifling of creativity. At least this was my personal declaration: I would do it in a way that would impact the communities to which I belong, and those I had yet to learn about.

Today, while I have yet to hit the pinnacle of success, modeling the aforementioned goal sets that the perfectionist in me strives for, I can say that I am getting closer. I am certainly more attuned to serving a greater purpose. I view my current position as a managing writer and journalist for the city of New York as a valuable steppingstone toward this. It allows me to engage with community and learn and document personal histories and concerns that I then present to our governing bodies with the goal of increasing compassion and understanding for the communities they serve. I document what efforts are made to enhance our communities, and how these efforts work or fail to bridge gaps and instill a modicum of trust between law-enforcement personnel and communities of color. As I enter my mid-level career, I find myself trying to channel the wonder and determination that flowed so intrinsically during my younger years. Avoiding disillusionment in a society so overwrought with distraction and desensitization is an ongoing challenge. In a world whose systems, by default, work to dismantle self-love and self-knowing, authenticity in all of its freedom and opposition must also remain at the forefront of my work.

For that is what writing in its purest art form has and will always be for me.

KRISTINE RODRIGUEZ KERR

FIGURE 23.1: Kristine Rodriguez Kerr. Image by author.

"WHAT IS PROFESSIONAL writing?" As the academic director and associate professor for the fully online Master of Science degree program in professional writing at NYU School of Professional Studies, I get asked this question a lot.

Just over twenty years ago, the first time I answered the question "What is professional writing?" it was being asked by my parents.

I was an undergraduate student in my first year of a four-year, full-tuition scholarship, and I had just declared a double major: creative writing and professional writing. At the time, I was the first woman in my family to attend a four-year institution[1] and I was the first of my siblings to attend an out-of-state, private institution. An eight-hour car ride from my hometown, I knew that if I lost my scholarship, I would be stranded in another state and unable to afford another semester. Worse, I knew I would disappoint my parents, who viewed my undergraduate scholarship as my chance to build a secure (read: financially independent) future for myself.

For my parents, a creative writing major was detrimental to their "secure future" aspiration. I imagine they were suspicious of the professional writing major as well. But they trusted the promise of their 18-year-old daughter when I told them in 2000, that I was certain I would be able to find fulltime employment after graduation as a professional writer.

Being honest now, I'm not sure that my 18-year-old self really believed what I told my parents or whether I just really wanted to be a writing major. I do know that the double major gave me the credibility to study writing and have my parents' tenuous approval. At 18, I certainly didn't know what I wanted to do *after* graduation, and I don't recall thinking deeply about it. What I did know is that I wanted my studies to stay rooted in words, in notebooks, in narrative arcs, in drafting and redrafting, in falling in love with phrases, and in anticipating my readers' journey.

By the time I finished my undergraduate degree in 2004—after several internships and a semester abroad—I had moved away from creative writing, recognizing that I was better at documenting the real world than creating characters. I didn't need to create my own stories when I could pull facts from the world and make them into something new and useful. I enjoyed the challenge of learning about new industries, interviewing subject experts, organizing information, and finding ways for niche and novice audiences to engage in a topic.

In striving to capture the real world in compelling ways, there was no lack of creativity in my life. More importantly, I believed in what that creativity and my role as a professional writer could do for a company. I stayed at my undergraduate university to complete a fifth-year Master of Art degree program in professional writing and was employed as a full-time marketing writer months before graduation (keeping my promise to my parents, much to their relief).

It was in this first full-time marketing writer role at a growing financial technology (fintech) company that my career began to overlap with education: in particular, the teaching and learning of writing. In 2005, shortly after I started at the company, the writing team was asked to develop training sessions for new hires and current employees on how to write better, focusing on helping to improve emails and messages to clients. These practical writing workshops became very popular within the company and soon I was traveling to different offices across the United States to hold in-person, week-long, writing workshops for software engineers, sales, and client-services teams.

In repeating these workshops across the country, I realized that many of my colleagues were very uncomfortable with writing although their jobs depended on it. This was shock. I had just graduated from an academic bubble of writers and was surprised that so many smart and accomplished individuals avoided writing because they believed they were bad at it (a self-fulfilling prophecy for many of them). Writing made them feel vulnerable, yet they had to write every day to clients, coworkers, and other companies. I realized in teaching these professional workshops that there was a tremendous disconnect between the styles of writing these individuals had learned in school (high school and postsecondary education) and the types of writing they needed to use in their careers. The years they had spent writing five-paragraph essays and academic papers had failed to prepare them for everyday, professional writing scenarios. Worse, their experiences had made them feel anxious and fear judgment every time they put words on a page.

After several years, many writing workshops, and a year as a high school English-language learner teacher, I returned to academia to learn more about the teaching and learning of writing and what could be done to fix this disconnect, which unfortunately still persists. In 2008, I was accepted to a doctoral program in communication and education within the

Mathematics, Science, and Technology Department at Teachers College, Columbia University. I've often said that teaching and writing are parallel endeavors. Both involve shaping information for a specific group to take up in new ways—the difference is in the timing.

In my doctoral program, I was introduced to qualitative research and was instantly drawn to the thick, rich descriptions involved in documenting the everyday, lived experiences of participants. Perhaps finding this work an authentic extension of what I enjoyed about writing as an undergraduate student, I lost myself in observation notes, seeking to capture every detail of interaction with research participants. I believed in what my role as an engaged observer and professional writer could do for building deeper understandings of phenomena in the world.

It was in my work as a qualitative researcher that I realized the activism embedded in my drive to create. As part of a research team, I began working with youth in the juvenile justice and foster care systems, seeking to understand their lived experiences as they navigated institutions of school and justice in and across New York City. For ten years, the *Reimagining Futures: Digital Arts and Literacies Project* documented the complex, lived realities of court-involved youth in an afterschool, alternative-to-detention program. In that time, during and after my doctoral studies, our research team had advocated for raising the age of criminal responsibility in NY State from 16 to 18; pushed for reforms of rigid zero tolerance policies in public schools; and sought to emphasize and reduce the disproportionality of minority youth in the juvenile justice system by drawing attention to unconscious biases, systemic racism, and exclusionary discipline practices.

In addition to the connection between research, writing, and policy changes, I wanted to empower my participants—young people in the juvenile justice and foster care systems—to tell their own stories in their own words. Again, my endeavors as a writer and as an educator merged and I began to run creative writing and storytelling workshops at my research site, documenting participant interactions and supporting practical writing skills. From 2009 to 2019 in these workshops, I sought to position creative writing and storytelling practices as a way for youth to make themselves, their experiences, and their beliefs known. Pushing beyond skill-based orientations, I invited participants to reflect artfully across online and offline spaces that included forms of posting, note- and list-making, as well as other modes of expression in addition to pen-on-paper writing.

Working with these youth has been a tremendous privilege and I am endlessly grateful for the time I have spent being creative with them in the afterschool programs. More than capable of telling their own narratives, the writing workshops became a place to encourage participants to share their own stories with larger, authentic audiences. In running these workshops, I am continuously struck by the range of creative pursuits, openness, and humor of these young people, who are too often described in ways that reduce them to their court-involved status. Although they might not initially realize the value in their out-of-school writing, these young people are combining words, images, and video (often in sophisticated and playful ways), across social media accounts, fan fiction sites, discussion boards, and in journals of lyrics, poems, and daily musings. I am heartened and remotivated in this work every time a young person who initially told me "I don't like to write" brings in a notebook filled with ideas or shares a website that they contribute to actively. My hope is that honoring and amplifying their workshop contributions is able to shift the perception of these youth as subjects to be acted upon and controlled because of their court-involved statuses, to an understanding of these youth as individuals with complex lives who should be involved and engaged as collaborators in their own education and development of future trajectories.

A big part of these workshops that is also part of answering the question "What is professional writing?" is expanding the definition of what counts as *real* writing. Too many creative individuals have lived the in-school disconnect that values formal, classroom writing over less formal, everyday writing. The consequence of this is that too many young people and professionals don't see themselves as "writers" and don't value the nuances in producing nontraditional texts. New composing and publishing tools (that allow for words, images, and sounds to come together and also make it possible to link digital spaces with printed documents) have created new habits in the way we communicate. For better or worse, these new communication habits are shaping our society.

We live in a text-saturated world and professional writing is all around us. Many professional lives are steeped in words, but not enough individuals identify as writers. We are living in a time when written text is produced and consumed at a rate never before seen. Countless individuals are spending hours a day (sometimes all day) with their hands on keyboards crafting messages for known and unknown others. Some of these writers feel confident and some feel very vulnerable.

As a professional writer, a qualitative researcher, and a teacher of professional writers, I believe it is important to recognize the writing work that individuals are contributing to the working world. It is also equally important to align writing education with the types of writing individuals are increasingly accountable to produce. In an era of fake news and divisiveness, professional writers have power and the rhetorical choices we make can work to increase understanding or keep information hidden. Company websites, online publications, and digital services are growing in number, sophistication, and readership every day. This has increased the demand for professional writers that can create timely and accurate copy across traditional, digital, and multimedia experiences. Preparing confident writers with the skills to ethically craft strategic copy for companies and clients across industries is critical because the stories we choose to craft and the ways we choose to tell them matter.

Note

1. My mother worked as a registered nurse in the state of New York for over 40 years before retiring. At the time she earned her nursing certification in the early 1970s, she was required to complete a two-year program. At various times in her career, she considered returning to school for a four-year degree, but never did—prioritizing the needs of her three children before her own education goals. As her only daughter, I grew up with stories that balanced regret for herself with limitless hope for *all* her children. Over the years, in numerous conversations I have tried to temper my mother's "less than" narrative, pointing to her long and meaningful career—which she proudly acknowledges, but never without a hint of longing.

MAAZA MENGISTE

FIGURE 24.1: Maaza Mengiste. Image by Nina Subin.

I AM WRITING this by hand on a warm night in July 2022. For the last six-plus years, most of my initial ideas and thoughts that have grown into anything worthwhile have begun this way: by opening a notebook and setting pen to paper. I started doing this when I couldn't see my way out of a writing nightmare. I had written a draft of my novel, *The Shadow King*, and the draft simply wasn't working. It was stilted and lifeless, and I didn't know what to do. The novel, set during Benito Mussolini's 1935 invasion of Ethiopia in order to colonize the country, had required an intense amount of research. As I flipped through the hundreds of pages of that first draft, which I'd dutifully typed then printed out, I saw my characters moving from one predetermined event to another, highlighting certain battles, locations, and sites. They were enacting history, rather than *living* in a historical moment.

Growing up in Ethiopia then eventually America in the 1970s and 1980s, I had heard incredible, breathtaking stories about the 1935 conflict between Fascist Italy and Ethiopia. The images that ran through my mind merged with ancient, epic myths I read in school, stories of Achilles and other defiant characters charging at a stronger, but slowly weakening, enemy. I wanted to write about Ethiopia and Italy's war with the same breathless energy that had overtaken me while reading *The Iliad*. I imagined my fighters, dressed in white, rushing down jagged hills while raising their spears and rifles against tanks and uniformed men with advanced artillery. I envisioned frenetic, heart-stopping scenes of heroism and defiance. Yet, the scenes I had written were sluggish. My characters seemed to drag themselves across historical terrain with effort, their every line of dialogue falling flat, weighed by details they needed to explain to the reader. After years of work, the draft was, in short, a dismal and distressing failure. Somewhere along the way, I had lost my sense of excitement about my story.

I had begun *The Shadow King* with a charged feeling that I will call inspiration. I was in Italy, at a desk, on a sunny April morning in 2011. All around me in that library were artifacts and photographs of the 1935 Italo-Ethiopian war. What I felt was a surge of kinetic mental energy—unformed but powerful—that was nearly impossible to ignore. I wanted to harness that energy to put what inspired me into fiction. I wanted to get a closer look at what it might have been like for people to have survived a military confrontation that many historians call the first real battle of WWII. I thought this *feeling* constituted an *idea*. I thought that this driving energy could propel me from chapter to chapter in such a way that events would fall into place seamlessly, unmarred by hesitation and clumsiness. I imagined that those events that fell into place would spring from historical documents and family stories and that as the story continued, that unformed but powerful energy would seep into every word and ignite each scene. I counted on inspiration to fuel more inspiration, but during the process of putting my ideas into words and trying to meet a deadline for the manuscript's submission—a date that I had already pushed back more than once—it all fell flat.

There was something I had wanted to put into my writing, some intangible but very real thing *between* the words that would have made the words pulse, so alive that they stretched off the page to envelop something grander than a sentence. But I had written with my brain, that container of facts, and there was nothing of the *felt world* in which my characters existed. I was also years late on this book. I had written under the pressure of time. That pressure had drained me of the focus I needed to expand my vision into developed thoughts and concrete moments. I had simply hurried into the writing without first pausing long enough to figure out what it was that I wanted to examine through this book. Inspiration, I was starting to understand, is not an idea. It is only the first nudge in a longer journey. But what is an idea?

For artists, an idea resides in that rich terrain that accrues meaning the longer a project gestates. I have often thought of it as an unsettled, unsettling question that each artist grapples with from project to project. It is something borne out of life that drives an artist to her desk or her canvas or her camera. An idea often starts to make itself known through a detail that we encounter, perhaps randomly, perhaps by searching, that ignites our imagination. That first spark of the imagination leads us toward those "rabbit holes" that researchers often decry while reveling in the exhilaration of new discoveries. And in those discoveries are contained new details that develop and enrich the anticipated story.

My quest to learn as much about this war and those men who faced Mussolini's fascist army in 1935 led me from one new detail to another. Yet, despite all my research I had forgotten a key element of writing a novel: Intrinsically connected to the development of a story must be both ongoing curiosity and flexibility to move where the story leads. This is the beating heart in every creative endeavor. And it was this that I had lost. I had stopped searching for discoveries, and instead paid attention only to those facts that could support what I thought I already knew. I had focused on those men who faced a more advanced European colonizing force. I had not seen the women standing next to them, I had not known how to look so that I could see them. I had not thought to sit quietly with the growing breadth of knowledge I was amassing in order to untangle the knotted realities that made up this particular conflict. I thought I was in danger of losing another most essential component of writing: time.

Ancient Greeks had two different words for time, *kairos* and *chronos*. *Chronos* represents what we have come to define as "time" in modern English, it is progressive and quantifiable: seconds, minutes, hours, days, months, etc. *Kairos* is a bit more elusive. It refers to those uncanny or carefully crafted incidents (or speeches) when the perfect words or event happen at what seems like the perfect moment. For example, when Amanda Gorman recited her poem, "The Hill We Climb," during the inauguration of President Joe Biden and Vice-President Kamala Harris, her appearance on the stage as a talented, young, Black woman reciting her verse for the swearing-in ceremony of America's new president captivated the world. But she was significant in other ways. While her poem was undeniably moving, her magnificent appearance and self-possession, only two weeks after the January 6, Capitol Hill attack and two months after the electoral defeat of an openly cruel, racist, and misogynistic president rendered her presence and her words even more potent. For a brief moment, the fear that had bound us all to our screens disappeared, and what we felt around the world was a steadying hope. Tucked within its *chronos* (time and date) was that elusive *kairos*. One can be pinned down on a calendar while the other carries a resonance that ripples out with sociological, cultural, and psychological importance.

When I was struggling with *The Shadow King*, I started asking myself what *kairos* and *chronos* meant to me as a writer. I am a historical novelist and in the most concrete way, I work with time. It is a path that I never imagined for myself; I did not know any writers growing up. I did not take a creative writing course in college. I was not surrounded by conversations about literature or the arts as a child. I simply liked to read, and I read voraciously. Books helped me travel to ancient Greece and China. Stories transported me to early 1900s Palestine and Egypt. I could be one place and still firmly rooted in another, my imagination making the connections to bring those worlds together for greater meaning. I eventually went to New York for an MFA but books and their writers, and how those writers contemplated history in relation to fiction have been my schools, my teachers, my mentors: James Baldwin, E.L. Doctorow, Han Kang, Toni Morrison, Gloria Naylor, Dasa Drndic, Alba de Cespedes, and many more.

Each of these writers illustrated in their own way how time is a pivotal element that defines the parameters of the novel. I took their lessons seriously, and like most of them, I focused my writing on a specific moment in time, in the past, from which I could glean new insights about the present. But that 1935–41 conflict, when it enters the lives of Hirut, a servant ordered to follow the Ethiopian army and care for the wounded, and Ettore, an Italian Jewish soldier who brings his camera to the battlefront, should also contain seismic changes: *kairotic* moments. If I am doing the work of the imagination, then writing is also a process of discovery that takes me again and again to the *kairotic*. What I mean to say is that for Hirut and Ettore (and all my characters) hidden in those chaotic calendar days of war were transformations that were breathtaking for their ability to outpace the immediate moment and transcend them. This was the essence of the story, not the war. What could I do to find the *kairos* within the story?

Those heroic figures of my childhood stories were my entrance into this historic moment. They were what led me to the doorstep of this war, and in many ways, into family memories. But I had not found the personal transformations that social upheaval inevitably causes because I had been too focused on the nature of the upheaval itself. I had not stepped close enough to my characters to see how their interior lives were altered, and how that, in turn, might have altered the course of this historical moment. So, I decided to step back, and in a sense, force time to stand as still as I could. But how to do that? How to tug at a moment and hold it still long enough to identify the invisible terrain of the human psyche? I worked backward, going through old notes, dog-eared books, magazines, and newspapers until one old 1935 clipping caught my eye. And this changed everything. The headline from the *New York Times*, September 11, 1935, read, "Women's Legion to Fight at the Front for Ethiopia." The article detailed the women, several thousands of them and from across the country, who were offering to join the front lines.

What would I do with this new discovery of women enlisting to fight against Fascist Italy? Here is a small detail: even as I am writing this, I am growing impatient with myself. The warm July evening is moving closer to midnight. My thoughts are tumbling out faster than my hand can move, and I want nothing more than to rush to the computer and furiously type these words out. But if I did that, I would miss the other kernel of information that is nudging itself forward, trying to gain prominence in the discussion about slowing and freezing time: my work with photographs. So I will tell you this right now: In order to force myself to slow down, to rid myself of the fear of deadlines and false urgencies, I moved away from the computer and started to write by hand. I wanted to strip time of its power and see whether a different pace could lead me toward *kairos*. I wanted to get in touch with the movement of my hand and allow an idea to develop, then flow onto the page.

I took out a favorite pen (later, in 2015, I would move to fountain pens but that's another essay) and a notebook and started to write what had first inspired me to take up this story. Some of those men I had once imagined rushing down rocky hills transformed into women running toward Italians in their long traditional dresses, shouting as loud as the men beside them. And as I jotted down one possible scene after the next, now centering women fighters, I kept coming back to Hirut, this servant who is also an orphan, but who refuses to believe she is worthless. I let her roam in my imagination and told her that I would follow her lead. She swept past the kitchen where she worked with the cook, past the sitting room she cleaned every day, and stood in her dark tiny room and held up her father's rifle, the only inheritance she had from two deceased parents. "I am a soldier," she told me. "A soldier."

In the midst of my deliberate notetaking, I started to think about the photographs of 1930s Ethiopia that I possess, images made by Italian soldiers while they were in Ethiopia. I had been collecting those images for over a decade, initially guided by nothing more than a deep interest in a history that was also part of family lore. There were scenes of my novel that I had

FIGURE 24.2: Unidentified young woman, Ethiopia, c.1935. From the author's personal collection.

reconstructed based on physical details from those pictures: the uniforms, the weapons, the terrain. Those photos had frozen time long enough for me to stare and learn. But in relegating them to tools for excavating a historical moment, I had deprived myself of the transcendent possibilities that might rest within the frame of every picture. I had looked at those photos to understand a period in time, but I had not considered that those photos also contained clues to interior lives: those of the photographed as well as the photographer. I would never have realized my own myopia if I hadn't forced time to slow. If I hadn't taken control of how *chronos* unfolded for me, I might never have encountered the potential of *kairos* in every photographed moment, particularly Hirut's.

On page 267 is a photograph that I might never have noticed if I hadn't decided to focus my attention on that invisible landscape just at the edge of our visual world. It is a picture of a young woman, turned away from the camera. Her eyes are slightly downcast though the set of her mouth implies both a smile and something else, an untapped strength. She is in a stained dress and her hair is braided with care. She is aware of the camera, and whoever is pressing the shutter wants to capture those aspects of her that I, too, want to see more clearly: her face, those straight shoulders, her upright stance, as if she will soon walk out of frame of her own accord. Her arms are at her side. She is not afraid of this Italian who is taking her photograph, this Italian who is part of an invading force. There is an entire universe in this image, a world where she exists, commander of herself, keeper of all that she claims as her own: a fighter.

Scene: Hirut, the servant, balancing her father's rifle in her hands and learning how to shoot, on her way to becoming a soldier. How does a female servant become a soldier? When she leaves the battlefield, does that young soldier become erased in the company of men who are also soldiers? What does it mean to be a woman in war?

I started my novel again with new questions.

MAX S. GORDON

FIGURE 25.1: Max S. Gordon. Image by Diego Santos.

SEVERAL SUMMERS AGO, in 2020, I went to a friend's house for a lunch party and the conversation came up around the question of whether books had become obsolete. With so many bookstores closing and electronic books available online, the answer seemed simple to my host: Books in print as we knew them were dead. When he observed the stricken look on our faces, he chastised us for being sentimental and reminded us that media have changed throughout history, and one form is often replaced by another. People always initially hate the new media, but they get used to them. That is just the way of the world. Some of us, myself included, acknowledged that while electronic books were more accessible, we outright refused to get used to reading everything—and especially novels—on a screen. My position was a bit hypocritical, as most of my long-form essays are published online. But I write essays to be read in book form eventually, and whenever I read a novel, I prefer a book in my hands. In my experience, books have been sexy, dusty, mildewed, funky, fragrant, torn, creased, used, brand new, almost in pieces, or wrapped in factory plastic. I love books from old bookstores, books found in charity shops, books at yard sales, books sold on blankets on the streets of New York. Antique books kept behind glass that requires a store-owner's key or dug up from the bottom of trash.

One of the first adult books I ever read I found in a dumpster near our apartment building in 1977. My friend and I, both 7 years old, were "explorers" digging for buried treasure. I ripped open a bag of trash and discovered, covered in cantaloupe rinds and eggshells, a mass-market book, the kind you could buy at the supermarket near the check-out line. The book was titled *Woman Doctor*. A doctor was fighting sexism at the hospital where she worked—from both the bosses and the staff—and I was here for all of it. As I sat on the couch reading, my mother asked, "Where did you get that book?" I was thinking, "Fuck *The Cat in the Hat*. This book is really good."

In 2021, my husband read *Berlin Diary* by William Shirer. Shirer was a foreign correspondent during World War II, and the book is his journal from 1934 to 1941, recalling his experiences with Nazi Germany. It's terrifying how contemporary Shirer's insights are on fascism, given where our country is now. I wanted to read the book at the same time, and found an inexpensive copy on eBay. When it arrived, it was in beautiful condition, and turned out to be a first edition. I opened the cover, and inside it read, "December 3, 1942. Happy Birthday, Dad, and many, many, more. Your son, Ray." I started to read the first page and realized I wasn't just thinking about the book or Shirer, I was thinking about Ray, and his father, and what it meant for someone to have read that book in 1942. I know books on iPads have their conveniences, but you can't get "Happy Birthday Dad. 1942" from a computer screen. Or the way the book smelled of attics or basements when I opened the cover. I wondered if "Dad" had read it, and if, when Dad died, Ray gave the book to his own son or daughter, what journey the book had gone through—not to mention the journey of the writer—to be held now in my hands.

———————

As a writer, in ways I can't fully describe, I see bound books as part of the witnessing experience. Books are mystical for me, an invitation to engage with someone else's world in a very specific way. My love of bound books, however, doesn't mean I fear that our desire for telling stories is in any way endangered. Whether it is the 5-year-old child rushing home from school shouting, "Guess what happened at school today?" or the co-worker pouring a cup of coffee in the break room and saying, "Chile, you'll never believe what happened on my date last night," the power of the story is what keeps you watching one more episode of the series you know you should turn off because you need to get up for work in the morning. Everyone wants to know happens next.

We also want to know: How will our own story end? This is the question we can never fully answer, which is why reading someone else's story, held between two bound covers, gives us a feeling of control: a beginning, a middle, and an end. The powerlessness of never truly knowing what will happen in our own lives and the inevitability of death inspire us to keep reading; it's the reason that storytelling and witnessing will always be essential to the writer, and especially to the queer writer of color. However I feel about printed books, of one thing I am sure: For some of us, it costs everything to get our stories told.

———————

I believe it is important to know where you've entered history, why telling *your* story matters. I am aware when I am writing that I am Black and gay, and that, to the best of my ability, I have a responsibility to tell the tale. I don't think it is hyperbole to say that stories can save lives. If you have any doubt, read the first chapter of James Baldwin's *Another Country*—his writing has often saved mine. Some writers are established enough to have another writer complete their unfinished work after death, but too many important books die as incomplete drafts in desk drawers or computers, in notebooks hidden away, or as an idea in someone's head. I've lost friends who I believe had brilliant work that will never be realized. Death seemed to come midsentence. There will be other stories, of course, there are always more stories, but we'll never get theirs, and that matters to me. I imagine the people in the world who needed those stories to be told, which is one of the reasons why I never take a finished piece of writing for granted. I will sit in a room for days in the same pair of sweatpants and the same tee-shirt if I have to, up all night and most of the day, until a draft is done. Once it is out of my body, out of my head, in some form in which someone else can read it, criticize it, tear it apart or praise it, I feel a deep sense of relief. And I am always haunted by the pieces I fear will die inside me, because I don't yet have the courage to bring them forth, or because I still worry what "they" might think (even when many of "them" are already dead). Honest writing means constantly negotiating shame and one's history. I reflect on Baldwin daily, the man and the myth, where he came from, how he grew up poor in Harlem, his brief time as a child evangelist, and the people, both Black and White, who nurtured his gifts as a child. I think of his departure to Europe, alone, nearly penniless and carrying the guilt, as a major caretaker in the family, of leaving behind his mother and eight brothers and sisters—he might as well have been going to the moon. As a writer, I appreciate the elements, the divine alchemy which had to come together for that particular witness in the world when so many other "James Baldwins" are destroyed by our society every day. I am compelled to ask, "What do I have to say about what it means to be a Black gay man in America?" That's what legacy writing and witnessing truly mean to me: a determination to write, to whatever extent I am able, in a way that will do for readers what Baldwin's work has done for me.

Sometimes we are so busy trying to survive, we simply can't write; racism, homophobia, sexism, class inequality, all forms of social violence, don't give you much time to reflect, to go from the literal to the symbolic—which is what a writer requires. Or we aren't disciplined or ruthless enough about our time, protecting our silences, which are sacred. We sit down to work, restless and mocked by the unwritten page, and end up taking the call from the friend who is breaking up with his ex for the fifth time and needs to "talk." Writers can be so overwhelmed by life we find it impossible to record it. Some writers are gobbled up by addiction. Every writer needs sanctuary, refuge—a "room of one's own"—even if it's only a few minutes in a crowded house standing behind the bathroom door.

But when everything comes together and we get a novel like Zora Neale Hurston's *Their Eyes Were Watching God*—a book with a living, beating heart—or Toni Morrison's profound and radiant *Sula*, we can celebrate the triumph of creativity over circumstance. That's true of any artist's work, but especially when you are Black or queer in America, when you have to deal with gender and sexual orientation and race and class and ableism. If you are telling the truth, there is no way in the world you haven't faced some serious shit getting those words on that page. Whenever I doubt the work, or myself, I just have to turn on the news to see the statistics of murdered transgender women, or read about another gay child who has been beaten or killed by her or his family for their sexual orientation, or who has committed suicide, to remind me that my work as a witness isn't done.

We know that most writers, whatever our experience or background, have many of the same voices in our heads: "Who told you that you could write?" "You'll never finish this book"; "None of this is working. This is garbage." What astounded me when I went through Baldwin's papers several years ago was that, even with fame and recognition, sometimes these voices remain. Then there are also the voices more specific to our identity: "No one will want to publish a Black writer on this subject." "Who wants to hear a queer story?" Or there is the even more personal warning: "Don't tell anyone what happened in our family." The good news is that wherever these voices come from—and there are so many—the writers we admire heard them and still found a way to the page. They got the work done and we are all the better for it.

When it seems that "they" want to shame you for your audacity, for your believing that your story is worth witnessing even to an audience of one (because all writers write first to an audience of one), that's when you must tell the world: This is what I saw when I looked out *my* window. If you don't like it, tell us what you saw when you looked out of yours.

———

A German woman who lives in the United Kingdom, a psychoanalyst whom I adore, went to a bookstore in 2021 and asked for Baldwin's *Another Country*. (Many times she has reminded me of the character Cass in that novel.) She could have downloaded it to her iPad that morning, but she wanted a copy in print. I loved the idea of the two of them meeting in his work, and imagined, from what I know of his friendships, that, given her inquisitiveness and generosity, he probably would have liked her. What sustains me as a writer, what compels me to write each day, is the presumption that there is someone out there, encouraging me, someone I have never met, who is waiting for my story, who loves to read and who will one day hold the weight of my book in their hands. I will be gone, and that person may not even be alive yet, but if the work lasts, as every writer hopes, there is a place where we will meet, in their consciousness and in my words. Despite the pain of writing—and sometimes there is so much pain—the anticipation of that unique friendship is delicious.

ODU ADAMU

FIGURE 26.1: Odu Adamu. Image by author.

Dry your eyes
Please don't cry
You can be strong
If you just hold on …

Ms. Winbush, I love you dearly. You have composed some of the greatest contemporary soul classics. And as much as "You Don't Have to Cry" (René & Angela 1986) is a forever jawn, the thinking behind these lyrics is what has us out here trying to be the Incredible-Super-Wonder-Panther-Man-Woman Person. At some point you need to cry. How can you hold on for strength when you need the strength to hold on? Who's to say crying isn't a sign of strength?

One of the benefits I enjoy living with HIV is a stockpile of medication. In addition to the components for the perfect "cocktail," I have pills to help me relax, sleep, and feel no pain … they're like the cherries that garnish your drink. I lined up about 20 bottles of pleasure on the coffee table and pulled out an unopened 1800 anejo, tequila reserva. Well, I had been "reserving" it for a special occasion. And I figured my last drink ever was about as special as shit would get. So, I got ready to crack the cap when … wait a sec. Let's back this up to give you some context.

November 2019, I decided I wanted to write and produce a television series. I had never produced a show, nor worked in television. In fact, at that time I wasn't doing anything TV or film related. But I knew I wanted to produce a show. So, I developed an idea; pitched it; and got a greenlight to move the show to development. Just like that! Easy peasy! Well …

The show had a Black LGBTQIA2SSGL+ (and whoever else we are by the time you read this) theme. And since I'm a Black, gay man the network thought they should pair with me a Black, gay senior producer. I mean, of course … don't we all know each other, or at least think alike? Note to folks who ain't us … and folks who are us: We ain't the same! Here was the issue.

The Black gay senior producer would request things. I would send them. And when we met, it was clear he never read anything I sent. Here was the other issue.

We would discuss things. He would go meet with the wizards. And all of the sudden, he didn't remember anything we discussed, so he couldn't answer their questions.

Then there's this: He told me he was getting pushback on my first three show ideas. Then, coincidentally, they popped up on another show about a month later.

People say I live "unapologetically." I just call it "living." I successfully pitched the show because I was clear. I'm Black. I'm gay. This is what I do. BOOM! He was kinda like: "I'm Black, but …" "I'm gay, but …" "Well, sometimes we need to …" He just wasn't the muthafucka who could rep. So anyways …

Even with all of this, we were able to move forward and come to an agreement for the series and pilot. We set a date to sign contracts. A brother was thinking, "Oh, I'm about to do my thing!" Our signing date was March 12, 2019, but there was this crazy little thing called COVID that had people questioning what was gonna happen, so we decided to wait about a week. And then it happened: On March 22, NYC went on "pause." Now wait, you mean to tell me the city is shutting down? Yup. Next came the email: "Dear Odu, Based on the blah, blah, blah." Basically, we're putting the brakes on your show. And how much did I have in my account then? About $28 and some cents. Ain't that some shit! What the hell was I gonna do?!?

As the days went on, the magnitude of this situation really hit. I had $18 and some odd cents (yes, I spent $10); rent was coming up, and everything was shut down. Any possible work I would have gotten was put on hold, and we had no idea what was happening next. I did know I had a royalty check coming, and that would cover April expenses, but what the hell after that? I held on for about three weeks, and then I broke. One of the benefits I have enjoyed from living with HIV is a stockpile of medication. That's right; this is where y'all came in …

I was about to crack the cap when a text came through. It was my ex asking if I was coming to watch *The Masked Singer*. See, we live in the same building and created a COVID bubble. I decided it would be cool to have one last moment with him and the Mouse, or whoever was still on. But when I got to his apartment, I just started sharing. I told him I was tired and ready to just end it all. I don't think he knew how serious I was, but he said something to me that totally shifted everything. He looked at me and said, "Don't worry. You know everything always works out for you."

See, I didn't call anyone because most of the people I know are useless in these moments. That sounds fucked up, but it's true. The reason is that they want to remind me of how strong I am. They want to tell me how much I can handle. They want to let me know if I couldn't handle it, God wouldn't have given it to me. They want me to "hold on," but don't offer anything to hold on to. They're basically "Don't cry" -ers. But my ex, who is not a person who goes deep or spiritual or new thoughty or anything said, "Everything always works out for you." He focused me on the reality that I don't have to do it all.

Something else is working things out. It's not about my strength. It's not about my power. It's about THE POWER. He reminded me about faith. He reminded me about trust. He reminded about knowing, knowing "everything always works out for me." But most important, he reminded me to realign with A GREATER TRUTH. As long as God is breathing through me the universe has a purpose for me, and I get to enjoy the journey of discovery … if I choose to.

And that's the thing. It's my choice. So, what was I gonna choose? I went back to my place after whoever was unmasked, gathered my little orange bottles up, and put them back in the medicine bin. Put the 1800 back on the bar. And I began to imagine.

I thought about the different shows I wanted to create. I became intentional about being well, being whole. I hunkered down in prayer, meditation, and affirmation. I now keep a gratitude journal and do things that bring my joy. I watch more comedy than tragedy and have taken a social media detox. Sometimes, I cried. And I started doing something else: writing.

I have been writing all my life, in one way or another. And my writing has been criticized for most of my life, in one way or another. It started with my mother. She was an English teacher and wanted me to know everything before I started school, so I was writing around age 3, and hearing about how I should be better than I was—from age 3—and how she didn't want me to embarrass her—from the age of 3. From kindergarten to eighth grade, I attended private school. "Penmanship" was a thing. "Cursive" was a thing. And being left-handed wasn't a thing. I worked extra hard to hold the pencil the "correct" way. I worked extra hard to have "pretty" handwriting. At least I was smart, so what I had to say was interesting, well, at least until high school.

I went to one of the academically highest-rated schools in the United States at that time and was enrolled in accelerated classes. I had attended the same school for nine years where I easily rose to the top and held it down. Now, I'm somewhere where everyone is … the top. Yeah, you already know where this is going. I did fairly well, even graduated with an A average, but it was hard ass work, and I struggled with English class. Well, it was one particular English class … and one particular English teacher. There's only one way to say this: Mr. Plummer was a bitch. He was a mean, catty, bitter queen whose life passed him by, and as his student you had to suffer for his losses. When he critiqued my work, I felt small and stupid. But I didn't take it personally. He was the same with everyone—students, his colleagues, even his son. Yup … his son … but that's for another time! The thing that really tore me down was he was exactly like my mother, and of course, they got along swimmingly. If Mr. Plummer wrote "This is dumb" on a paper, she affirmed it without even reading my work. [It's as if the red ink from his pen erased my words. By the time I graduated I was over the idea of writing. But I wasn't done with writing.]

    I have a Bachelor of Arts degree, so you know that means four years of consistent writing. Almost every job I ever had involved writing: staff reports, protocols, proposals. If it's technical, I've written it. I've written published articles. I have been a ghost writer. I wrote a book on Black gay men and kink—literally! And every time I wrote something I would hear Mr. Plummer in one ear and my mother in the other, kinda like the devil on one shoulder and, well, the devil on the other. Because of this, the process of writing was intimidating. Whenever I had to write I was filled with angst. While I was doing it professionally, I still avoided being called a writer. I also stayed clear of writing opportunities. And I would NEVER write for myself. You couldn't get me to journal to save my life. But home alone during the pandemic I realized I needed to get things out of my head, so I started writing. And with everything going on in the world, I started writing more. I went from just writing about how I was experiencing life to social commentary. I started sharing my writing on social media. I started attracting people who wanted me to write. I delved into prose and shorts; gained a following. WTF?!?!? I asked myself, "How come this is happening?" And eventually, I was able to answer …

    When everything shut down on the outside, I was able to shut some things down on the inside. Not dealing with the world meant I wasn't answering to the world. I could do what I wanted how I wanted, and I started writing how I wanted. Left to my own devices, I kinda write like I talk (which you've probably figured out already). It would never fly at any of my professional gigs, but it was well received in the social media universe. It didn't matter if everything was perfect, what I was saying was being received, and shared, to the point that my writing landed in the hands of a writer I hugely admire, and I am currently writing for his site.

Releasing my thoughts around writing opened much of my life. This took my mind off the money I didn't have, and that's when my money started coming in ... from everywhere: royalties, gifts, a couple of good ole guvment dollars, and even unclaimed funds! A couple of months later I created my own production company: ROCK MY SOUL Media, LLC, and started producing virtual programming. I didn't need to wait for a green light from anyone; the universe gave me the green light. This opening also created the opportunity for me to write scripts. My work led to me being selected for a documentary intensive cohort, and in January 2022 I released my first film, *Body Language*. The film explores body image and experience for Black, gay, queer, same-gender-loving men. And it's my film, directed, produced, edited, and WRITTEN by me.

Currently, I am working on my next project and exploring creative endeavors outside of filmmaking. But none of this would be happening without that moment. Don't get it twisted; the past two years have held many moments. And it ain't been easy. Sometimes I get outta my spiritual thang and let the world shit takeover. Then, I check myself, get back on track with my practice: prayer, meditation. Sometimes I cry. And cry some more. I am still writing, and somewhere in all this I realized I enjoy writing. I even journal!

Full transparency, I had one other moment when the pills almost came out, but they didn't. But when I got the thought this time, I went to the biggest lesson I learned last time: "I don't have to do this alone." When I needed it before, what I needed came from someone else. Someone else reminded me, "EVERYTHING ALWAYS WORKS OUT FOR YOU." Here's the thing, most of us have gotten caught up in this independence trap.

"I can do it on my own."

"I can't trust nobody."

"When I really need someone, no one is gonna be there."

Whatever the dang reason that's keeping you from reaching out needs to be released. LET IT GO! I was able to get back in my groove … with support. And maybe the most important thing: I took responsibility for telling people not to tell me I'm strong. That attracted people who let me go through what I needed to go through, when, how, and for how long I needed to.

"You don't have to cry
alone.
I'll pull you through these times
and help you hold on …"

That feels so much better. By the way, I still have the full bottle of 1800. I'm gonna be here a bit longer and have a lot more special occasions coming my way, so no need to rush.

Reference

René & Angela, (1986), "You Don't Have to Cry," *Street Called Desire*, USA: Mercury Records.

ROSS BERGER

FIGURE 27.1: Ross Berger. Image by Yfat Yossifor.

High School

I became a writer through high school theater, where I failed as an actor mainly because I couldn't remember my lines. I couldn't relate to the words of old-timer playwrights, as I hadn't lived through the Industrial Revolution or the Spanish American War. And, really, could there be anything less interesting for a 17-year-old? So, I started fudging the scripts to adjust the lines to my conversational style. This is pretty much forbidden in theater, but in high school, the standard isn't dictated by a review from the *New York Times*; rather, I was performing for my friends, and if I didn't shine in front of them, they could be more vicious than Clive Barnes.

Despite the protests of many stage managers, I did find a home for my lack of discipline in the summer of 1993, two months before my senior year. I joined a theater group of teenage actors who would write and perform social-oriented sketches for high schools across my home state of Connecticut. We all got paid minimum wage to act in the playlets that we wrote. *How is that not the perfect high school job?* I soon discovered that it was the writing, not the acting, where I felt most at home, most complete. Writing was not to become a hobby, but a profession and obsession. It was exhilarating to connect an audience to an actor through the words that I wrote, and all I wanted from that moment forward was to replicate that feeling through this new craft, and it didn't have to be for the stage. Any medium would do. With that commitment at age 17, my professional goals were clear. Little did I know the path to achieving them would involve endless hardship, rejection, and penury that never fully goes away.

Even with ample opportunities to leave writing, I've discovered that I can't. Lines of dialogue flow through me randomly throughout the day, as do unique pairings of words that hope to be part of something bigger. When writing the first act of *Death of a Salesman*, Arthur Miller was typing at such a feverish, breakneck speed that he felt less like a writer and more like a stenographer for his imagination. This is often true for most writers I know, even if the work isn't up to snuff (which it isn't most of the time). When the imagination takes charge, it's not something I can dial down; it's a curse that I just gotta give in to.

In other words, writing is not a profession that I chose; it's a profession that chose me.

The Great Compromise

I'm most realized as a writer when I write for myself. This should come to no surprise to anyone; the average writer will say the same. But I genuinely struggle to write for others when the task at hand (often copywriting) requires no depth of emotion or thought. I just can't "hook" into some invisible muse, or trigger a cognitive mechanism upon command that elegantly pieces words together to describe the most mundane things.

This isn't to say I can't fake it. I'm just not good at pleasing a million masters who are either uniformed, capricious, or both. The result is often diluted tripe, or worse yet, empty letters on a page or screen that are *pro forma* adornments and exist for the sub-1 percent of people who actually read what's there.

These types of jobs, whether they're in the field of advertising, online marketing, user experience, or technology, might employ hundreds of thousands of people, but the primary task at hand, despite what the job description says, isn't writing; it's wordsmithing. It's a rarified skill, yes, laconic and clever, but often devoid of genuine emotion or intellect.

To understand, to prove, to seek justice, to educate—this is writing—be it for art, journalism, activism, the classroom.

To persuade someone to buy a product, to instruct someone on how to use a product, to describe a product—this is wordsmithing—be it for commerce or … just commerce, really.

Writing can pay the bills, but not often, and such a privilege is reserved for a lucky few. Therefore, most of us writers rely on wordsmithing jobs to make ends meet while we continue to pursue our book, play, or screenplay. To make the hours of the day as least painful as possible, I've discovered that my wordsmithing roles must be as least taxing as possible. A good relationship with a boss, easy content to wordsmith about, less churn on edits, a short commute—all of these are important to prioritize when one chooses their next opportunity.

One of my biggest regrets—and it's one that reappears either during financial hardship or pure avarice—is taking a high-paying job that compromises my personal writing. The daily stressors of meeting product deadlines or client demands, particularly in the tech world in which I've often found myself, can take over my life absolutely. It is a mental regime change that installs new priorities and values that erode my commitment to my artistic passion. There simply isn't enough time in the day to write and serve a corporate monarch. I know people who have done it. Few have lasted long, most have taken years to finish a book or screenplay, and of those, their artistry diminished profoundly. But the overwhelming majority have either given up writing completely or have left their corporate job for a world of employment volatility but artistic gratification. Of course, there are those who tire of the chase and cannot face another rejection from a publisher or producer, thus entering the corporate world is a legitimate improvement over their current circumstances. This is more than understandable. However, if one had committed themselves to the life of a writer, this moment is a mournful one. That life is now over.

I dread this moment. I think about it all the time. Being a writer has defined me for over 30 years. To say goodbye to it is to perform the impossible. My endurance and my ability to balance financial pressures with artistic satisfaction are greater strengths than my ability to write, and they are likely why I do what I do. If either one was to fall, particularly my endurance, then it is obvious what decision needs to be made. And it is one that will be made for me.

Nocturnal Creature

Sinatra was right.

When I lived in New York pursuing an MFA in playwriting, I could finish a draft of a play at 3 a.m., make a copy of it at Kinko's, take the subway to Midtown, mail off the copy at the 24-hour post office on 34th Street, go to an outdoor kiosk, buy a magazine, and read it at a nearby diner by 4:15 a.m. while waiting for my eggs and bacon. These days were the most thrilling of my writing life, being one with the periodic stillness of an electrifying city. I felt privileged that I knew a secret about New York that few people did. At 3 a.m., there is light in her darkness and a quiet vitality, far removed from the bustle of eight million people who set foot upon her every day. It was an unusual period for me, the early 2000s, one that cannot be duplicated, mainly because I was a student then and had no responsibilities to a loved one or a full-time employer. Nonetheless, I learned that if I wanted to remain a nocturnal writer, I needed to live below my means and find a job with a flexible schedule to accommodate my writing life.

After graduation, I found part-time gigs and short-term assignments as a copywriter and editor and, eventually, as an adjunct professor and speechwriter. In early 2002, I lived in Brooklyn, deep in Midwood, in the house of my grandmother, who had been residing in a nursing home after suffering from a debilitating stroke. Within a few months of my living in that house, she passed away, a little more than year after my grandfather did. Built in the 1920s, the three-story house, which my grandparents had called home since 1944, had a massive hole in its roof and was falling apart in numerous places. It was dusty in the way that old houses are: No matter how many times I vacuumed the floors or cleaned the tables, everything seemed coated with a permanent sheet of soot. The walls would aspirate nanoparticles of detritus like pollen from an oak tree. Despite this, it had the nostalgic charm of 1940s America. Living there, I often imagined Jack Benny echoing from the kitchen radio, the afternoon paper delivered onto the brick doorstep, and kids playing punch ball on the street. I'd jump right back into present day once I headed toward the Q train on Avenue J and East 15th Street, and within two blocks, I could hear seven different languages: English, Urdu, Russian, Arabic, Hebrew, Yiddish, and Spanish. This was a different kind of New York; this was Brooklyn. Not the insufferable Lena Dunham Brooklyn filled with the transient hipster enclaves of Boerum Hill or Park Slope. No. This was the real Brooklyn, centered on either immigrant families or those with deep ancestral roots to the borough whose children would be educated in a local "P.S." and who'd be forced to accept disappointment as a way of life when it came to the Mets, the Jets, and the Knicks.

None of my friends would have lived in that house, but as a struggling playwright, I was grateful to do so rent-free. There was a single provision, however: My father and uncle required me to clear out sections of the house week after week to prepare it for sale. This was no small feat. The endless stockpile of empty bottles, clothes, newspapers, and ceiling plaster comprised 50 percent of the volume of stuff that needed to be discarded. The other half, the more important half, consumed more of my time and bore a toll on me that I didn't come to grips with back then.

That other half was the purging of 60 years of Depression-era trinkets, half read books, water-stained letters and pictures, and other familial residue. I didn't question then why my grandparents didn't make any effort to clear out much of these non-essentials from their house while they were alive. Nor did I question why my father and uncle didn't call a professional junk removal service to do my job and place the house for sale within months of my grandmother's passing. I was just happy to have a home. It wasn't until I had to do the same, with a much smaller collection of my non-essentials, upon moving apartments on the West Coast, nearly 20 years later, within a month of the COVID epidemic shutdown, when I truly understood the power of nostalgia.

For my grandparents, such trinkets and letters represented a history of living through the Great Depression and World War II and the raising of their twin boys—moments that defined them, moments that could never be replicated. Upon my grandparents' deaths, the baton of nostalgia passed on to their two sons, but for them, they would not be saying goodbye to the memories of the Depression, World War II, or twin sons. Instead, they would be saying goodbye to their parents. When I first moved into that house, this was a task neither son was willing or ready to take on. As I understand it today, my living in that house served as an essential convenience for my father and uncle who needed time to build up the strength for that final farewell. I was oblivious to this back then, regrettably, being too selfish as a young writer, as young writers often are. The memories of living there remain with me to this day, but they are not mine alone. They are, more so, my father's, my uncle's, my grandfather's, my grandmother's …

Gradually, I realized I could not sustain a long-term future writing theater, taking up short-term gigs, and living in a house frozen in time. I shifted my focus onto television after having written an aired episode of *Law & Order* in the fall of 2004—an opportunity that came about after an actor friend of mine introduced me to one of the show's producers who was open to fresh ideas from playwrights.

A year and a half later, in early 2006, I mustered the courage to leave the city I loved so deeply for a city that I didn't love at all—Los Angeles (LA). An agent who was a fan of my episode told me there was more work there than in the East Coast. I listened intently, thinking I was going to become the next David Chase or Terence Winter. Instead, my first year or so in LA was defined, once again, by struggle and financial hardship, and culminated at the picket lines of the 2007–08 Writers Guild of America Strike. What little momentum I had up to that point quickly vanished, thanks to a five-month, industry-wide work stoppage. I asked myself repeatedly was the move worth it? Is this career worth it?

Game On

The 2007–08 Writers Guild of America Strike didn't prove to be a victory for the Writers Guild, despite their assertions after the fact. Television networks filled their channels with reruns of dramas and comedies and with reality TV shows (which hire "story producers" in lieu of writers) *ad nauseum* and still made a killing with advertisers. Everything went back to normal quickly once an agreement was made between the union and the studios and networks, but there were some quiet disruptions that made an indelible impact on the industry, namely the rise of digital content on YouTube, the emergence of Facebook, and the use of the smartphone as a TV screen. It was clear to me that the future of entertainment did not center on television or film, but on emerging technologies that have their own platforms to tell stories: smartphones, online video sharing apps, video games.

Eventually, in late 2008, I found consistent work in the video game world, which was significantly more lucrative than editing and copywriting. Games allowed me to be an unencumbered storyteller. With the faith and trust from several development teams, I had autonomy in developing characters and plot, driving home themes, and working with actors during voice over sessions. Games were not my first love, unlike cinema, television, or theater was. Nevertheless, games allowed me to be the type of writer I had been training to be, and there was no Hollywood cronyism or endless spec script charade for my work to make it to the marketplace.

After fifteen or so years, I find that my craft is validated by players across social media, Twitch, and YouTube. To get better at my job, I read the criticism as well as the compliments. I am no longer writing in the shadows, playing the Hollywood game where talent seldom wins out. My work is out there, entertaining millions of people. This is not why I pursue writing in this field, nor does it drive me today, but it is a reminder of the impact writers can have and the responsibility to keep getting better for the next opportunity.

This is a far departure from my days as a playwright, toiling away amid the paint chips of a neglected house in Midwood. But never does a day go by when I don't use the past to fuel my imagination to solve creative problems of today. Heroes in games, be they NBA stars or sci-fi travelers of broken timelines, need an all-consuming drive to move forward in a story. What is it from their past that has seared a redemptive imprint on them once the game begins? How do they confront the skeletons of their past when solving the main conflict of the game? Video game heroes are no different than heroes in books, film, or TV. I approach them as people with a genuine pain or profound absence. Can the pain ever be solved? Can the absence ever be filled no matter the mission they are on? Likely not, but that is not exclusive to game protagonists. No hero is ever completely fulfilled spiritually or cured of their pain, but they get closer to managing it, to closing the gap once a story is over, and it is their emotional journey in doing so that makes them aspirational to players who attempt to do the same in their own lives.

Compelling characters come from heartache, and lived experiences and courage are the writer's only tools in making these characters genuine, no matter the medium.

The Constant Pivot

My approach to creating compelling characters isn't confined to video games. Whenever I see a new technology emerging, I often identify leads on LinkedIn, cold call tech companies, and offer my skills for a chance at freelance employment. Is there an opportunity to tell stories on their uncharted platform? If so, what do I need to learn to tell a great story on it? These pivots to new technologies occur every two years, and this journey has taken me to the stage, TV screen, mobile devices, user-generated content (UGC) platforms, video games, virtual reality, augmented reality, conversational artificial intelligence, e-books, print books, magazines, and hybrid media. One might argue that I'm someone who can't sit still, and they wouldn't be wrong. But I have not changed crafts wholesale. I'm still a writer. But the medium through which I tell my stories changes periodically, and I must learn the grammar of that medium to tell the best story that I can in it.

I must admit the hustle can be exhausting, and what is often asked of me can diminish my skill-set. Yet, I march on to learn something new, to get paid, to get better at my craft. And yes, there are moments when the corporate virus spreads and tempts me to surrender my personal writing life. I can give in ... but just a little. My new habit prevents me from doing so all the way. Short stories are a new medium for me, and writing them transports me to my early days of writing plays. It's been a freeing process so far, one that pays dividends—four published stories from 2019 to 2022. It cleanses my palate, purging the bad after-taste if I'm working on a regrettable idea from a non-creative executive for such-and-such tech product. The writing keeps me honest, keeps me harmlessly selfish. I can't cheat on a character motivation or force a plot point if I'm not trying to impress anyone, if my audience is just myself. Also, there are no graphics, special effects, or an actor's performance that my words can hide behind. The experience I create is on the page. What happens in the exchange from my words to the reader's eyes leaves me defenseless. Regardless if the work is good or bad, that defenselessness is my version of the all-consuming drive. And that defenselessness drives me to write each and every day.

SAMIYA BASHIR

FIGURE 28.1: Samiya Bashir. Image by Nina Johnson.

Overheard

The trouble with arrival is how it feels
so finite:

>Journey toward destination,
>then arrive,
>then the end.

>Journey complete.

My own experience is of beginning again. And again. And again. Not from scratch each time, which is the real gift, but more like a builder, more like a twinkle-textured disco-ball Jenga set, journey and arrival spin above my head—where every bit and shard can come crumbling down at any time—
>and does so
>each time I pull a foundational piece of
>structure.

But—sometimes—that itch—that tight skin—must—pull!

I'm the eldest child of a mother who is the eldest child of her mother. I spent most of my little years surrounded by grownups who talked about grownup things and lived their grownup lives all while I—silent and usually unseen—watched, listened. Strong sense memory stories include an embrace of quiet invisibility and its helpmate: piping up to go along for the ride. I'd slip across a back seat and disappear into overhearing.

To grow up was to know all the ways to catch snatches of things that I wasn't supposed to know yet.

>Thing is:
>>Structures aren't forever,
>>needn't be—for me, at least—shouldn't be.

To wit:
I left the Bay Area for NYC in the 1990s because I needed the kind of pressure that can shatter as well as shape. Whether true or not, at that time I felt that I could quite literally anti-grow as an artist and remain comfortable as a person. As an artist, celebrated;

even, brave, or some shit, no one, then and there, seemed to ask me that coal-crushing, facet-forcing Jacksonian query:
> *What have you done for me lately?*

So then—
> to shape or to shatter
>> perhaps a question more of when and where
>>> than of *if*. Sometimes, one must shatter. Often
>>>> there is often no other way
>>>>> to grow.

Making a life, for me, has always been a quest for time—through time—a wrestling with competing needs for both structure and time unrestricted. They seem opposites, but my consistent work is to figure out how to get them to live in concert.

To wit:
> Bill Bixby didn't become Lou Ferrigno
> without ripping through,
> shredding his every piece
> of clothing.
>> Never
>> not one time
>> was his Jekyll-fit
>> undisturbed. Safe.
>>> Same. Never,
>>>> not once.

Now, a thing that can drive a body to distraction is pain.

And, fact of the matter is, shattering hurts.

But, quiet as it isn't even kept, so does shaping and sculpting and form.

So does stillness and its often coincident rot—I think of the bound foot, of
> the clipped bonsai,
>> orthopedics and orthotics,
>>> levees which contain/constrain their rivers,
>>>> shape wear which constricts breath and matter
>>>>> not to break
>>>>> but to construct.

"IT'S ALSO PERFORMATIVE." That overheard sentence, which inserted itself into my thinking and writing with some kind of truth, is also true.

I'm not, like, anti-stillness—I just don't know her. But that's another essay I'll likely never write. Let's be real, I would be nowhere without it: stillness, its silence, its noise, its performance. And yet, here I am, tasked to consider whether and why any of it—my work, its maker—even matters.

**Thing is–I overhear but from the inside–
I gotta make new recent work.**

So, according to the literature, I'm a disordered eater. Food is both delicious and a horrendously arduous undertaking.

And it's like that, this whole writing thing. I can't exactly *not* do it if I hope to maintain even a moderate facsimile of sanity. Likewise, to maintain even a moderate facsimile of health—even, life—I gotta eat. No matter what the Soylent boys say. No matter what I'd rather do. I don't usually eat very well. But still, I've gotta.

I don't usually write very well either. But the Muse Industrial Complex makes certain guarantees. The more I write, the more some things makes sense—even if only to me; and if I'm honest, most of the world seems completely senseless, if only to me.

The thing about having no choice is that one *does* have a choice about whether or not to *share* what one leaks from one's being. Just because a thing needs writing doesn't mean it needs reading. Most things I write don't need sharing. That understanding, oh dear, I fear is like acting. One makes or writes or performs because one must. One shares because this time, this piece, this moment, might actually matter, to someone, someone else—that's the thing—someone, even, who you can't even imagine.

Even now, I look back on pieces I've written which I find literally cringe inducing—but that's, as my inner ego+id couple's counselor might say, *my* shit. Often I learn that whatever I want to burn is something so meaningful to someone else that I'm blown, like match flame, back to humility. Once returned, I'm reminded how much this whole business of writing, of sharing, is just not about me, and for good reason.

If I still stanned (in eons-old-already parlance) something I wrote 30 years ago in San Francisco, then I wouldn't be growing as an artist. Uncomfortable as it may be, my own artistic ontogenesis remains as essential as shedding old skin to stretch into the new.

Birthing? Cleaving? Extricating? Whatever.

All nerve endings, I overhear, and beauty.

As artists we are trained to lean into reverence for the ego at what seems to be every turn. But the work (Occam's razor?) leverages our labor to bring it into existence and then gallops off—or in—once made, on its own terms to live its own life (n) either with us (n)or despite us.

What matters to this writer then is *that* the work matters rather than *why* the work matters. Like my Black-ass life, one lets *why* get in the way; suddenly one is working to imagine or create the *why* rather than the *what*, rather than the thing itself. The work must *become* if it is ever to matter—like life.

AND WHAT AM I TO BE—<u>RAW OUT HERE?</u>
Entrails all exposed? Skinless?!
Nah, B! Nawwwww.

For most of my life I was the young kid in the crowd, friends and family near-universally older than me. Before we were so obsessed by generational actuarial tables, I was the perfect age to watch too many mentors die too young of AIDS and cancer and general neglect. Yes, that part. But also, there's me:

I'm a bit exoskeletony—lone-wolfy—
   a bit lionessy, yet
      a bit hidey from my pridey. Yet and

still, I learned to listen early enough to become an Olympic-level amateur overhearer. Still and yet through various mentorships—some of us, always June Jordan reminds, do/did not (yet) die—I learned the ways and how's which attend the work of listening.

For instance: Just get in the car. Pipe up to go along for the ride. I've learned more on many a store run than I have in entire terms of class time.

The people you admire? Those from whom you can learn? Be of service.

What I know is that I've gained more from fetching someone a drink or a tissue than from many a structured interview. We are all, in all ways, our asides.

These are among those ways to be with—to be in place to grow, to ether-learn, to overhear.

By this part of the page the night is long-legged and middle aged, like me, so I'll share a secret: Everything takes me a thousand times longer to do / to make / to become than it might seem. No matter the length of my stride.

No matter how many machines I manipulate. No matter what plethora of apps and screens, I keep finding in myself the need to pare down, to slow. Most of my writing gets done by hand—I'm trying to say—despite the wild digitalia of our world. Imagine. In this, the year of our capitalist clock 2,000 plus 22, it's strange to say, but stranger to realize, considering I don't do much journaling.

That's a lie, but only kind of. What it is, really, is a shame.
My life is kind of fascinating. ¯_(ツ)_/¯

But something about trust is missing there
where intention lives / lays / lies.

My mother has always, at least as long as I've known her, had the television on, the radio, the record player.

My sisters and me? It's the podcasts. The millennials among us can even make whole televisions out of phones sans annoyance or loudly acknowledged needs for emergency chiropracty.

So, I understand my mother's desire for sound, digital company, the comfort of conversation, even if it's only one sided. Even now, I write by hand, outside, surrounded by strangers in conversation. I may as well be in the world's back seat. Still too small to see over the front bucket seats, I peer through the middle by ear. And it's the best of both and all. No one is talking to me. I can listen or not. I needn't pay attention. But I'm also not left alone to my silence. Still.

And yet, I need it—that silence, its poetry. But
sometimes I also need it to leave me 'lone.

> **"That's the way," I interrupt the overheard speaker,
> "to do prison, I figure." "I got lot of fuckin' writing done,"
> she replied. Fait accompli.**

What does it mean to write with the never silence of breath?

> To write with space
> with absence and color—
>
> if I red a poem, how is it read
> by my color-blind friend?
>
> Does their sight
> newly right my stanzas?
> Rewrite my melodics?
>
> Does my red sound brown?
> Will it gray?

I have a friend who is, in fact, a great painter, a major artist, even. I like to wear the coats she no longer wears—her hand-me-overs. They always have paint on them somewhere. Not great art or anything, just drips and smears, leavings and stains.

And me? On occasion I can't help but write a poem. But on more important occasions I am able to sculpt poetry from the raw material of writing, reading, listening.

That's the *can't stop*. That's the must do. It's not as if I can't stop creating beauty or writing poetry or making work—it's actually remarkably rare that I do any of those things. But writing? It's a constant, like a tic, a twitch, a security blanket. It's like a dictionary for the only language I'm allowed to speak but am also, always, (s)training to learn.

SAMUEL R. DELANY

FIGURE 29.1: Samuel R. Delany. Image by Bill Wood.

§1. BACK IN the early months of 1982, I saw a preview of the movie *Conan the Barbarian* in which there is a really offensive queer bashing scene. The entire preview audience hissed. And in the film's plot, that obviously on some level was designed to be an "antisexist story," there were so many sexist elements that every time one came by, the audience hissed again.

But that was a time of great change. It was the Upper West Side of New York, a highly liberal area, and it was a time when some audiences, if they were sensitive enough, *would* boo something in a movie preview that was supposed to get their approval.

Another thing probably worth saying is that the bad politics in science fiction come from the same thing that bad politics in most art come from. And it's probably worth noting also, that in a number of areas the politics in science fiction are at least a step or two ahead of what's going on in the other arts. I think it's very important to remind people again and again, and also to remind the best-intentioned people, because they forget this—that what makes statements like "Blacks are lazy and shiftless"; "Women are lousy drivers"; or "Homosexuals are emotionally unstable" racist, sexist, and homophobic is not the statements' content, however wrong or ridiculous that content may be. What makes them racist, sexist, and homophobic is the vast statistical preponderance of these particular statements in the general range of utterances of most people most of the time.

It's the fact that such statistical preponderance makes it almost impossible to say anything else about blacks, women, or gays. It's the silences in the discourse such statements enforce around themselves that give them their ideological contour. And this is why you have to correct the statistical balance. This is what's wrong with people trying to censor such statements, in an attempt to right oppressive wrongs. You don't right the imbalance—the inequality—by suppressing discourse. What you have to do is allow, *encourage* even more: Intrude new discourse into the area of silence around these statements and broaden the subject. Then such statements just become comments about one or a few observed individuals, statements that are either right or wrong, silly, or interesting.

§2. Here's an old insight that I've said many times throughout my career, realized as far back as my first novel, which I wrote in 1961:

One of the best ways to portray characters is as a combination of purposeful actions, habitual actions, and gratuitous actions. And somehow the most insignificant male character almost always gets portrayed as a combination of all three. However, the same writers will find it absolutely impossible to portray women characters as exhibiting all three kinds of action. If the woman is an evil woman, she will be all purpose with no habits and nothing gratuitous about her; or if she is a good woman, she will be all gratuitous action and no habits and no purpose. It's a very strange thing. So, when I was writing a set of three books called *The Fall of the Towers*, I sat down and made lists of all three kinds of action for the women characters; then I would get to the end of the chapter and realize I just hadn't put them in. It has all the structure of a psychosis. It really does. When you discover that you are a victim of a psychosis, you realize just how deeply it works into the whole of society.

§3. The work we like to do is most easily done with pen and paper first, and eventually we learn how to do a fair amount of it with typewriter and paper, and then keyboard and screen; but at each step, we have to learn to do more with the keyboard that involves leaving signs on the screen of where, in a very small, very complicated circuit, we have left the signals that tell us where the text is now lodged.

§4. William Gaddis (from the novel *The Recognitions*, 2020: 260):

—My dear fellow, remember Emerson's advice, Basil Valentine said, and paused. There was a crash at the corner. From where they stood they could see that the cab had hit a bus.
—We are advised to treat other people as though they were real, he said then, lighting his cigarette,—because perhaps they are.

§5. I've always seen myself as someone with multiple talents—some nowhere near as good as others but visible when taken in context. For many years, I was not sure whether I was going to be a musician or a writer. I felt I was a first-rate arranger up until the week of my birthday in 1968. Till then, I'd felt there was an equal chance of my giving up writing and going on to music as there was continuing to devote myself to writing. But then I began the five years of work that took me all over the country and even to England (you can follow my travels in the place-date subscriptions to my novels *Dhalgren* and *Triton*) that represented a final turn to writing. In San Francisco, I directed a small film, *Tiresias*, that was lost in the mail. I directed a play in French. And I returned to New York (twice) and continued writing and making three more movies.

Thus, the question, "Why do you write?" seems oddly skewed. The only art that I more or less rigorously suppressed—except in moments of private self-indulgence—was poetry. Even then, sometimes I slipped.

§6. Have I directed for the same reason I've written? I'm not sure. Certainly I'm aware that some of the arts require more stamina and focus than I've been able to give them, and as I've grown older and physically weaker, I've certainly given up filmmaking and gone back to writing.

Why?

Is that a reasonable way to frame the remainder of my attempt to answer the initial question: "Why do you write?" Let's assume it is.

§7. I am still deeply unhappy with the way I speak extemporaneously in public, which is, again, my bow to one of my writing masters, Theodore Sturgeon.

§8. *The Iliad*—the Story of Troy—is a far more complex poem than *The Odyssey*.

It is not so much about a war as about the way the squabbles among the Greek tribes, including Achilles' tribe, the Myrmidons, lead to the destruction of a city at the rim of Asia Minor. The Anger of Achilles, we are told in the invocation, is the topic of a complex tale. And who is Achilles? He is a gay, and possibly transgender warrior in a tribe that maintains "an army of lovers" much like the Spartans hundreds of years later, who does not want to fight, but whose honor has been offended by the withholding of a slave girl named Briseis, and he will not fight, he tells his own lover, Patroclus, until she is returned …

When Menelaus came to demand he fight alongside him, Achilles dressed in women's clothing and retired/hid among his women. Somehow Menelaus discovered his female name and called him out—that name is not told in the tale. But in his book on poetic magic, *The White Goddess*, Robert Graves opined that with a little sleuthing it can be retrieved …

In situations where no single person could have the big picture, *The Iliad* might have been translated as "The Greek Squabbles" (rather than "The Trojan War") and how people who might have had the larger picture, Cassandra or Laocoön, were tragically ignored and thought to be magicians.

§9. When I was in the sixth(?) grade, I had the great fortune to see the English actor Michael Redgrave (I was taken by my friend, Peter Ascoli) in the American Performance of Jean Giraudoux's extraordinary anti-war play, *La guerre de Troie n'aura pas lieu*, in Christopher Fry's elegant translation (*Tiger at the Gates* [1955]). It helped make me a pacifist; a paraphrase of the near-climactic lines still stays with me: "On the eve of the war, the generals of both sides meet and confer and explain to each other that war would be the absolutely worst thing for both sides—yet all creation *knows* they'll go to war!"

§10. *The Iliad* and *The Odyssey*, along with French playwrights such as Giraudoux and Sartre and Anouilh, were passions of my early elementary school days, starting in the sixth and seventh grades. Many years later, during the time I lived with Frank Romeo, I came under the influence of some people in New York, whom I went to for six weeks or so, who had a course in meditation that involved "letting go." There was a man and a woman and a dozen or so of us who would sit around a table, and we would practice a kind of relaxation therapy, in which we would work on *not* wanting anything. The logic was something like this: If you could convince yourself that you did not want it, then you would enter the emotional state you would be in if you had it. Although they did not talk about its Buddhist origins, certainly I recognized it as a basic Buddhist approach to freeing oneself from the wheel of desire. I didn't stick with it very long, but it was very useful, I think, in getting through some of the trauma that accompanied my relationship with Frank, which I have written about in other places—largely on Facebook in my Notes.[1]

Shortly after these faux Buddhists, I began work on my autobiography, *The Motion of Light in Water*, and I found myself flooded with early memories, which I tried to write down. Basically *Motion* takes me from childhood through my first trip to Europe, and as I wrote there, up until then, my life had been remarkably chaotic. But now I resolved to be a lot more stable; I was living with my toddler daughter. I hoped my life would cease to be interesting and my work would become more interesting. This was the situation I lived in for the next 40 years, in the same apartment, at 184 West 82nd Street.

This was the case until, finally, I accepted my son-in-law and daughter's invitation to move down to Wynnewood, PA, on September 10, 2015.

Over that 40 years such works as *Hogg*, *The Mad Man*, *Phallos*, and more substantial works such as *Dark Reflections* and *Through the Valley of the Nest of Spiders* now materialized, along with films such as *The Orchid*, *Bye Bye Love*, and *The Aunts*.

§11. Often today, the prospect of writing, especially when it's a matter of answering questions that I have answered before, strikes me as unbearably exhausting. A week from this particular date (April 29, 2019), I have been asked to go up to New York City and take part in something that could conceivably be of interest, but because so much of it is retreading things that the people who asked me were inspired by in work written almost 20 years ago or more, right now doesn't strike me as very interesting. I can only hope that when I get to the venue and talk to the largely younger people who will be involved something will move me to articulation. Right now, it entails going to the 42nd St. area and standing in front of the sites that have since been torn down and reading from *Times Square Red / Times Square Blue*. The man who is organizing this has picked out the sections, and I have just marked them in a copy of the book that I plan to take with me to read from.

I had an editor friend named David Hartwell, who, indeed, was my best friend in the science fiction community in which I made my living for many years, and who himself, I felt, was an extremely important editor in a field where the editors proved again and again to be the heroic people who contoured the field's history. He used to say that in all his years as a professional editor, he never published anything without finding, within the first five minutes when it came back from the printer, something that was amiss with the text. Myself, the realities of publication have always been some kind of disappointment for me, for much the same reason. The writer often feels like Sisyphus climbing his mountain and rolling his rock uphill, hoping for a book where the print is not too small, and where there is no major typographical error within the first 10 pages. I suppose I write in some sort of blind hope that the book that appears will itself be a wonderful object.

Of course, what we writers get is a mass-reproduced text that, in one way or the other, is always inadequate—which is probably one of the reasons why we write again.

—September 9, 2019
Philadelphia, PA

Acknowledgments

"Samuel R. Delany" is an excerpt from Delany's book, *Of Solids and Surds*, which was published in 2021 by Yale University Press. It appears in *Artists as Writers* by permission of the author and the Bent Agency. © Samuel R. Delany.

Note

1. In 2020, Facebook abolished Notes.

Reference

Gaddis, William (2020), *The Recognitions*, New York: NYRB Classics.

SEPH RODNEY

FIGURE 30.1: Seph Rodney. Image by Francesca Magnani.

I'LL START WITH the question of when I began to properly write. Properly? Yes, properly. By this, I mean regularly, rigorously, systematically—to write and be edited and reconsider the writing in light of these edits. So, I don't mean journaling or penning long letters to friends and lovers which I also do. Proper writing began when I took Martha Rhoades's poetry workshop—I think in 1991. I'm not sure about the date, but I do know I was there for a couple years and stopped attending because in 1993 I returned to Long Island University-Brooklyn campus to work through my undergraduate degree. I had actually first attended college several years before at age 16, but fell into a series of depressions that made me lose some years; poetry and art helped me dig myself out of the deep hollows I fell into.

Maybe I was already writing on some internal scroll before the workshop. I had a sense of language being within my grasp from almost as far back as I can remember. I have a clear memory of this when I was school in Jamaica, before coming to the United States at age 6. In Jamaica at that time, it was normal to punish students by hitting them with a belt or a thin cane that teachers carried with them to remedy infractions large and small. We were hit sometimes for getting answers to the teacher's questions wrong. I remember being hit on my open palm I held out in fear and trembling for being late to school. But when the subject was English grammar, standing at the board in front of class where I would typically be as shy as a fresh bruise, I was confident, at ease with language, with its mechanics. It made sense to me. This became a theme for my life: I thrived where my facility with language let me enter a kind of flow state. There, I could show off my knowledge, while I shrank in other situations where I thought my intellect had no purchase.

I was initially afraid taking Martha's workshop. It was the first time in my life I had to consciously write for a critical audience. The way she ran the workshop was that each participant had to bring in at least one piece each week to work on. Then she always had someone else read your poem, and thereafter you would read the piece out loud for the group. This meant writing every week, whether I felt inspired or not. I had to write. It also meant letting other people pick apart what I had written, which in turn meant learning in my early 20s the crucial distinction between critiquing a person as opposed to critiquing their work. I'm grateful for this lesson. I don't think this is a distinction that the general public in this culture often makes. Years ago I decided that being able to make this distinction is a sign of emotional maturity.

Writing for that workshop also meant I had to learn to be strong on the page—as opposed to being strong in performing the work. This circumstance that went against the then current cultural grain of the early 1990s was when the performance poetry scene began to take off. For a while, when I lived in Fort Greene, I would flirt with that scene, reading my stuff at the Blue Moon Café, but I was never a performer and could only gingerly look up from the paper every now and again to connect to the audience. Being taught to be strong on the page was, now in retrospect, good training for me.

When I returned to college at 23 my training became technical. I worked for four years, from 1993 to 1997, in the campus writing center, mostly dealing with fellow students who struggled with issues of grammar, essay structure, and clarity. I recall often using the same strategy over and over to get the writer to more clearly see *how* they were writing, what assumptions they made, what they neglected to spell out. "Okay. I'm going to read this sentence to you." <I read it out loud.> "Now read it to me." <They read aloud.> "What does this mean?" Then they would explain what they were trying to say, and I would say "Write *that*. Write what you just said to me."

These were the easy ones. More difficult cases were ones like the woman who was already teaching in the New York City Public School system and didn't know what subjects and verbs are or what they do.

At this point in the story, I need to go back. I need to talk about *why* I wanted to write poetry. I wrote because I had read Sylvia Plath's *Ariel* poems (the last ones she had written before her suicide) and I have not since read a poet since who has more intimately spoken to me. Even 30 plus years later she still astounds me. As the fellow poet Robert Lowell said of Plath: "Language never dies in her mouth." I eventually stopped writing poetry because I didn't think I could get to where she had with those everlasting passages, like the one in "Mary's Song": "The ovens glowed like heavens, incandescent. / It is a heart / This holocaust I walk in, / O golden child the world will kill and eat." The first time I read "Fever 103°" at 16 (only because my mom had likely taken some literature survey class while earning her nursing degree at Hunter, so it was in our living room library) I felt that Plath lit a flame that has not gone out, and it won't go out until I do.

In college I mostly wrote prose, literary analysis, on my way to a degree in literature. I still wrote poetry now and again. I won a small poetry prize in 1995 for a poem I had submitted to a journal. It would take me about 25 years to win another prize for my writing—this was the Rabkin Arts Journalism prize which I won in 2020. This prize included a $50,000 purse, so it constituted more than just validation. It allowed me to move outside the city to a place with quieter days and easier sociality.

But the rigor was starting to develop in me in college in the 1990s. I started to train my writing muscles to write 10- to 15-page papers by holding the structure of the essay in my head, though I always taught my tutees in the writing center to write from an outline. Slowly, I started to get good at writing these essays.

Then I fell in love with art, took up a camera, began shooting in the studio, decided to go to art school, and got there: UC Irvine in California. There I wrote much less. I graduated after a brutal two years and then realized I didn't have it in me to be a studio artist. After that, there were several years in the wilderness. I worked retail, which at first I enjoyed. These jobs, at Hugo Boss at Beverly Center in Los Angeles and then later at Emporio Armani in Beverly Hills, were the first times I was paid relatively well for being a really good salesman, patient and charming. However, when I began to wither away from having no intellectual challenges, I got sick of retail. I tried writing but realized I didn't know how to do proper visual analysis, or how to carry out research. I wanted to write about art and knew I needed these skills.

I went back to grad school to get these. I moved to London and, worked on a PhD in museum studies, essentially from 2006 through 2015 (though I had moved back to New York in 2011). I wrote constantly, but mostly it was in a voice that I could mimic, but not command. I didn't really want to be an academic. I just wanted the skill set.

The whole time I was working on the doctorate, taking one crappy, demeaning job after the other, I didn't have a career in mind. I had no idea that the profession of art criticism could be open to me. But I dreamt about having meaningful conversations about visual art, and then sought to write for art magazines. Around 2012, I got a crucial opportunity to write for *Artillery Magazine*, which my friend from grad school, Carrie Paterson, who was an editor there at the time, helped me get.

I wrote 500-words-or-fewer reviews. They could not be one word over 500 and having this word limit made me disciplined. I learned to pack in meaning in this space, to describe lushly, to make the reader see what I was seeing, to convey the ways in which the work was memorable, or tortured, or drowning in its own insouciance. I learned to be comfortable with being rigorously edited. I learned I had a voice, and that it is poetic and innovative, and desperate to avoid cliché.

I essentially stalked the *Hyperallergic* crew for a year right as I was finishing my thesis in 2015. They seemed like the place for me. Eventually I became a staff writer for them in 2016 after about a nine-month courtship. I worked like a broke-dick dog to get six stories a week written. I schlepped out to Staten Island and other outposts on the edge of civilization, such as the Knockdown Center in Queens, New York, to find things to write about. Once I even drove up to a performance art center with a woman who had a peacock in the car that she kept as her pet. That trip I ended up having to sleep in what was essentially a barn (because the owners of the space tend to treat the artists they work with like dogs and they thought they could treat me the same way) and woke to bites all over my legs from the-devil-knows-what insects.

About a year and a half later I moved up to editor at *Hyperallergic*. At this point, I finally stopped being agonizingly poor—not just because of the steady salary—but because I began to get requests to write lucrative catalog essays. It was only in 2018 that I began to feel that I might be able to make a life out of writing about art. I recall a particularly important moment when I felt this way: I received a large check for an essay that allowed me to pay off my friend Lawrence who had housed and fed me in the first years after I returned to New York and was still working on the PhD I wrote him a check for almost $4,000 and felt like a real adult.

Since then, I've also been awarded the Andy Warhol Arts Writers grant and been elected to be a board member of AICA-USA, the local branch of the International Association of Art Critics. These accomplishments help make the previous 30 or so years of brutally hard work and constant immiseration feel like preparation. Since working at *Hyperallergic*, I've written for the *New York Times*, NBC and CNN, and have been on television for the Joy Reid Show and even the Jim Jefferies Show. I've also written articles and essays in which the language feels consistently alive and searching. I learned to use poetry within my art criticism, precisely because poetry is the language of attention and because I am attuned to its lyrical and contradictory beauties.

The mentors I had were many; Martha Rhodes was foundational. My political science professor John Ehrenberg, a proper Marxist, was an attentive and careful reader of the papers I wrote for his undergraduate courses. My boss at the writing center, Steve Newton, said one thing that stung and stayed with me: He said that I liked to "put a big red bow on things." I think I've stopped doing that. I recall what a fellow student said when I was on a summer semester abroad in Europe, with a university located in Florida. He told me "You're the kind of writer who doesn't like to write, but likes to have written." I still think about that. I think that's kind of true. Writing is still often agony, but now I know I don't have to always like it. Sometimes it is just work, and that's okay. Hrag Vartanian, the editor in chief at *Hyperallergic*, has been a kind of mentor to me as well, though the first years I was there he was, at times, impatient and emotionally brittle. Eventually we became close colleagues, and he has taught me more about how the art ecosystem works than anyone else. I am deeply grateful to him for hiring me and supporting my experimentation (I once wrote a poem as a kind of review and just a series of numbered questions in response to an exhibition by Kara Walker) and honing my analytical vision (my piece discussing my mistakes as a critic was spurred by a conversation with him). I think of what one past girlfriend said to me when she read some of the things I had written for *Hyper*: "You are gifted." Karoline, a lovely and kind German woman with a background in popular press, and later advocacy writing, made me feel that I really have it in me to write something that might set the world on fire.

I also think about a conversation I had with my father when I had come back from a disastrous first year away at college in Pennsylvania when I had begun to break down. He asked me what I wanted to do with my life, and I responded honestly, "I want to have good conversations." I did. I still do. And now, with the life I've made for myself, I get to have them.

STEVEN G FULLWOOD

FIGURE 31.1: Steven G Fullwood. Image by author.

Journal excerpt, August 15, 2021

Took some shrooms today at about 1:28 PM, waiting for them to subtly kick in. I'm on the couch watching Twin Peaks: The Return. *I want to decompress and swirl a bit. A belly full of cereal and oat milk. It's about 80°F outside. My cat Amsterdam Thelonious is sleeping.*

Black people + David Lynch. Not the best combo except for Nina Simone's exquisite "Sinnerman" and a troupe of limber Black dancers closing out the mesmerizing if confusing Inland Empire. *But mostly Lynch's Black people serve as background music to explain or embellish scenes featuring White people.*

Earlier, before I ate the mushrooms, I thought to myself that I would like to die off camera. That is, I don't want my demise to be a spectacle on social media. Just let me be la la la somewhere where there are no people. No hospital plugged in like the fucking Matrix. Fuck morphine. Instead, let pain riddle my body, let an angry cancer chew through my intestines.

Let my body rest. Let my body rest. Let my body rest … preferably nude. Let death's symphony complete its tune in a key only I can hear and can pay full attention to. At home, in my bed. Some stiffness, some rattling, coughing, and choking probably, and then. a. good. long. sigh.

That's the wish, anyway. Who knows what's coming or how? A set of electric, paralyzing strokes with the last one finishing me off? A crazed fool, a stereotype with a gun, spraying into a crowd in Harlem with me catching one fate-filled bullet? Or worse, just living a long, miserable state of being that I can't distract myself from with art or other people?

Death, how shall we greet one another? What will be my state of mind then?

* * *

Writing is the way I fend off death. It is the only constant in my life other than the inevitability of death. Since 2016, I've mourned the deaths of countless family members, among them my brother to chronic heart failure, 48 (2016); a nephew to suicide, 21 (2019); an aunt to cancer, 72 (2022); and my father to a series of seizures and strokes, 84 (2022).

Writing is the one thing I can bury my face in and scream and imagine something other than the terror of dying I've felt since I was a child. In my work I play with terror, ask death questions, make obscene jokes, seduce it into telling me things I can't hear otherwise in my usual frame of mind.

I often immerse myself in projects that I know I'll never finish. But finishing isn't the point. It's doing the work. Journaling keeps me accountable. Helps keep me present and relatively clear. Writing is the only place I can go to figure it out: life, people, my motivations, what I think I want from myself and other people.

Writing can be the place where you find out that you—as a good friend of mine put it—are *not* the hero of your own story, or that much of what you do doesn't really matter. I mean, it's fun and all. Keeps you busy, at least.

* * *

I'm not a great thinker. I write to create spaces in my thoughts. I need time to consider what I've done or what I need to do. I suspect there are lengthy pauses in dialogue in David Lynch's films and television work because … he wants you to listen. He wants … you to … pay attention. I need spaces to consider what I think and why.

Since I was 4 years old, I was always speeding toward a "whatever" in my mind. Writing slows me down, makes me take stock and provides a reflection.

I maintain a lifestyle of working independently that is almost always in flux. And the only thing grounding me other than exercising is writing. Exercise for my body because I tend to live in my head and throat and writing because there needs to be evidence beyond my lived experience.

* * *

I was born January 15, 1966, and raised in Toledo, Ohio, on the southside in Kuschwantz, a White-flight neighborhood that was one of two early twentieth-century Polish settlements. My parents, a Southern father (born in 1938), and a Midwesterner mother (born in 1940) both descended from farmers, domestics, factory workers, preachers, handymen, and hustlers. My dad, a chef his entire life, now deceased, once sang in a gospel trio called the Horns of Zion. My mother, an enthusiastic pink-collar worker who worked at a bank, a school, the Toledo Park Service, among many places in Toledo, also enjoyed sports and was a reader. She once told me that she would read anything if it caught her attention. Growing up we all knew that mom loved romance and horror books. Think Stephen King and Janet Daly.

I'm the third of five children, the pesky, bothersome middle kid with way too much energy. I grew up in a musical and literary household with lots and lots of television.

Like many writers in this book, I started writing to make sense of my life—first and primarily in journals. I forecasted my days by writing to-do lists, and recounted what I did or tried to do, which helped me as I struggled to become visible to myself. Later, writing became a way for me to pause, to stop talking and engage myself, to consider what I truly believed about this world and its possibilities. After decades of writing beginning in 1982 (and publishing in 1987) articles, essays, poems, lyrics, short stories, suicide notes, conducting interviews, reviewing films, books, and music, in dozens of journals, analog and digital, these stories mark time as well as exist in some quiet, timeless space of *I was here*.

The first article I ever wrote for publication was never published, even though I was paid for it. In my archive, I hold a check stub for $25 from the *Toledo Blade* in 1987 for an editorial I penned about the importance of Black history. I didn't expect to get paid. I just sat down one day and poured my feelings out about why I believed Black history mattered and dropped it off at the newspaper in hopes of it being published.

Maybe a week later, the *Toledo Blade* sent me a check and a note: "Thank you, keep writing," or something like that. I didn't save the note. I was shocked to get the check. At the time I was working as a waiter/cook at Pizza Hut in west Toledo in August 1984. Nineteen, skinny, and scared of everything but acting like I wasn't so I was *extra*. Mercurial, anti-social, and sometimes cold. Most of my money was spent on albums, musical instruments, food, and rent. After 18 years of living in a home terrorized by an alcoholic father, I left determined to become myself. That self was obsessed with being a rock star.

While others were starting college or working in offices or factories, I had no other ambitions other than becoming a rock star who wrote, sang, and produced himself. Fuck college. Fuck the army. Fuck the office. I was something special.

I read *Creem, Right On!,* and *Rolling Stone* and watched as much MTV as I could. My Walkman was always on.

1985, a year after graduation: I paid for piano lessons, but hardly practiced on my cheap Yamaha. I took singing lessons with a former opera singer who taught me Italian arias. I bought a used electric guitar from Durdell's on Central Avenue, a music store I used to pass by on my way to and from work at Pizza Hut. But I could never fully play it. Just a few licks.

Around this time, I also tried my hand at writing songs, scores of hard-to-sing lyrics. By that I mean the melodies of the songs existed only in my head and sounded terrible live or were strikingly like Prince's. Files of these lyrics, which I often combined into thematic "albums," accompanied with themes and images, are labeled, and neatly stored away in my archive.

What also remains from that bittersweet, sweaty hopeful time are a handful of printed photographs of me in rock star poses: holding a guitar; sexily dangling from a tree by one arm; smiling, bare-chested, with a bow tie and high-top fade at a dance competition at local dance club. I won one round but lost the larger contest.

Along with the article that was never published, this writing formed the foundation of my career as a writer and editor: those terrible, sexist, and unoriginal lyrics, those made-up sexual encounters, those tumescent teenage desires. But much later I realized I was learning to how to tell stories.

It's 2023. I have archived hundreds of essays, articles, poems, and interviews that I've published and thrice as many that I haven't. I mention this not because I am bragging—no. Much of that stuff is unreadable. I do so to illustrate my writing ambitions and my archival impulse, both which shape my literary life.

*　*　*

January 1996, I left Toledo to move to Atlanta for graduate school out of fear of disappearing or becoming a terminally depressed Black gay male with no future. While at Clark Atlanta University, I had an opportunity to work at the Library of Congress for the summer of 1996, and then returned to Atlanta to complete my degree. December 1997, I drove from Atlanta to Toledo, sold my car to my father, and hopped a one-way flight to New York. In February 1998, I took a job as an archivist at the Schomburg Center for Research in Black Culture. Back then, I was living in Morningside Heights near Columbia University. May 2000, I became a Harlem resident.

After nineteen years, three months, and 24 days (April 28, 2017), I left the Schomburg Center to pursue filmmaking and photography. Throughout this uneasy and sometimes painful transition, it was my writing, personal and professional, that has been constant and necessary through the midlife change from an employee to an independent worker.

In October 2020, I had the pleasure of presenting a virtual tour of Harlem to a small group of students at Columbia University led by Professor Shirly Bahar. I chose to present Harlem specifically through the archival collections of some of its notable residents, artists, and activists including James Baldwin, Audre Lorde, and Paul Robeson. The coda for my presentation were quotes by two authors, former residents, both intent on exploding the dream of the Harlem Renaissance in the world's imagination by presenting a sobering view of what it is/was like living day-to-day in one of the most famous neighborhoods in the world.

In novelist Ralph Ellison's essay, "Harlem Is Nowhere," written in 1948 and published in *Harper's* in 1964, the writer offers a dim portrait that could have been written in 2021.

"To live in Harlem is to dwell in the very bowels of the city," Ellison wrote. "It is to pass a labyrinthine existence among streets that explode monotonously skyward with the spires and crosses of churches and clutter underfoot with garbage and decay."

Sharifa Rhodes-Pitts, another writer, captures a transforming place in the thrall of gentrification in 2011. Her book, *Harlem is Nowhere*, looks literally at the remaining foundations of Harlem.

"As the empty lots disappeared, I became more interested in what was there before," Rhodes-Pitts (2011: 12) wrote.

> In some places it is possible to see what was there: the foundation of a building remains; a front stoop rises up from the sidewalk but leads to nothing. Such things recede into the background, part of the natural history of this place, as if they had always been like that. But this is the evidence of an unnatural history—it was not always this way; it came to be that way for a reason.

Garbage and decay. Churches on almost every street. An endless search for what was once there, real and imagined.

While developing my tour, it occurred to me that I too had a Harlem, one familiar to Ellison and Rhodes-Pitts's, but more expansive and uniquely my own. It is one that I will tell you about here because it's not only the place where I live and the background for my life as a writer, but is also the realization of a dream I dared to dream about when searching for a place I could call home.

From 2000 to the present, I've lived in Harlem in three different apartments among Astor Row Houses on 130th Street between Lenox and 5th avenues, which were built in the late nineteenth century by the Astor family as vacation homes for overseas visitors.

Although I didn't begin my writing career in Harlem, it was certainly realized and encouraged there. Much of my freelance work, running an independent publishing company (2004–15), serving as the editor of several anthologies, and working as an archivist and curator at the Schomburg, developed, enhanced, and cemented my reputation as a writer and editor.

I'm fortunate to do what I love for a living, and I can do it in Harlem. And no other place I've lived in or visited for work or pleasure appealed to me the way that Harlem does.

Harlem world was the residence or workplace of many of my literary and artistic inspirations. Remarkably my life as archivist afforded me the distinct honor of processing the personal collections of many of these people including James Baldwin and Lorraine Hansberry. As a Black queer man, Harlem offers a unique, fertile space for creativity and activism that is world renowned and immortalized in the work of Baldwin in the 1950–60s; in the Hamilton Balls (aka "The Faggot Balls") in the 1920s; and a former lodge in Harlem (the Imperial Elks Lodge) where the documentary, *Paris is Burning*, was filmed in the 1980s.

My Harlem pulsates with wonder, delight, and mystery. For me it's a research center, museum, and arts salon surrounded by stunning parks, Queen Anne, Romanesque, neo-Classical, Neo-Gothic, brownstones, and other kinds of exceptional architecture. There is always a charming coffee shop or restaurant within walking distance, as well as a very active sidewalk culture, bustling nightlife and basically everything one might need (grocers, laundries, churches, theaters, culture centers) if one doesn't want to leave the neighborhood.

And my neighbors, for the most part, are kind and hardworking and hail from just about everywhere on Earth. And for more than a century, descendants from Africa and her diaspora have inhabited Harlem shaping its sound, taste, appearance, and politics and being among Black people from everywhere matters to me.

Harlem is easy to get to by several train lines, buses, or taxis. Great for bikes and simply wandering by foot through its remarkable streets.

But like many other internationally known neighborhoods, Harlem is also a place in flux, perpetually reeling from the city's negligence and, more recently, the ongoing damage caused by the pandemic. Shuttered businesses line the main thoroughfare. Homeless people tote bags of plastic bottles and aluminum cans and rummage through garbage receptacles or slowly push shopping carts of their meager belongings. You can't walk down the street two blocks without being besieged by people asking for money or food. During the throes of pandemic, it wasn't uncommon to see drug addicts shooting up in broad daylight or splayed out against abandoned buildings. Even now, I see the effects of the war on the homeless, the poor, the mentally ill and drug addled by Mayor Eric Adams' administration.

My friend Sean calls 125th Street—one of the most famous streets in the world from Lenox to Lexington avenues—"the artery of addiction."

Upturned public garbage cans on street corners. Dog shit smeared on sidewalks. And a daily motorbike brigade.

And all that and it's still home. Early during the throes of pandemic in the spring of 2020, I surprised myself with an epiphany. While at Central Park North sitting on a large piece of schist overlooking the Harlem Meer, a thought came to me. *This is where I want to be. This is where I need to write. Harlem is the place I plan to live until I die.*

Of course, there might be other suitable places for me to live in the United States, or possibly overseas. But I am no longer interested in searching for them. You see, my 57-year-old aging body craves a base. My mind wants familiarity and security in real time so I can be wilder in my work and imagination. My heart declared Harlem as my final resting place.

This is my home. And I have writing to do.

Reference

Rhodes-Pitts, Sharifa (2012), *Harlem Is Nowhere: A Journey to the Mecca of Black America*, New York: Little, Brown.

SOFIA MAIA CIEL

FIGURE 32.1: Sofia Maia Ciel. Drawing by Karina Beumer.

1.
November 2017
He asked whether I have a dream. I replied straight away: *No.* Precarious lives don't have dreams. I mean they do, but dreams about having health insurance, the place you feel you belong to, being able to predict the next day, get some rest, read the *New York Review of Books*, and do simple things which many people take for granted are not real dreams. Or are they?

You need to have a dream. Everyone has a dream.

There was a long while of silence and when I broke it saying under my breath, *I want to be late for the plane*, he gave me that strange look like I didn't understand the question. I repeated with a lower tone and certainty in my voice:

I want to be late for the plane.

2.
Carolee Schneemann once said that she started to paint before she started to talk. I could say that I started to write before I started to talk, but maybe it was also because I barely talked. My father was always wishing me the very same on every possible occasion; *and it would be good if you start saying something.*

The reality was too much. Sounds were too heavy.

In most of the cases, pronounced words require a presence of another person, and a person in most of the cases expects an understandable referential function of language (as Jacobson would kindly notice).

Does she have a problem with speaking?

I didn't, but what was the point to speak? Written words were different.
Scribbles, side notes, endless notes on the margins and papers. Papers everywhere.

I was never thinking whether I want to write or not.
The words were falling out asking to stop whatever was on the way just to get out of my head—a curse and a relief. More of a

curse, but then in the midst of the impossibility of writing, it was even worse. Writing is a cursed relief. Period.

3.
In August of 2003, I was 22. That year I decided not to come back from my usual summer job in the United Kingdom and sent a blue-ink, handwritten letter to the dean officially taking a year away from my "Eastern-European" university.

These days were waking up early, preparing and serving breakfast for the guests at a three-story, seaside hotel in Aberystwyth, cleaning the hotel quarters and greeting the newcomers. In this repetitious routine, there were the titles of the books and newspapers in people's rooms. The view of something less superficial than *The Daily Mail* made the start of my day promising. Most of the time I did the cleaning together with a lovely Welsh lady, and when I pointed meaningfully at a book, she said with this blissful smile and characteristic accent *Yes, my love, I read that one too; it is the good one!* Straight from the hotel to the diner-like place, just in time to jump in for the lunch rush hours and stay there until the late afternoon. Most of the all-day breakfast eaters were reading the *Sun*—if reading seems applicable here. With my usual *Be careful, with the plate; it is reaaaally hot* the platter landed on the infamous page three girl.[1] From there I went straight to my last job for the day at an art gallery—where finally I could relax.

I usually fell asleep as soon as my head crashed the pillow. It was tiring but fun as well, new places, new people around. In your 20s you have a lot of energy and think of time in a different way from later on, having at the horizon something magical: a future.

Maybe one thing in that situation was a bit irritating—my physical incapability of absorbing any long texts. (I do not even mention writing.) Every time I saw a person reading a book while I was making coffee or wiping a table, I thought: *soon*. However, the horizon of *soon* felt still *far away* and I wanted something *sooner*. Found it. When I think about it now it seems absurd, but if the absurd makes you feel better? You just do the absurd. I asked my mum to send me my heavy, clumsy book for learning ancient Greek.

I must say, I should really be thankful to my mum that she never questioned my wired pleas and instead of asking *Why the hell?!* she was like: *Ohh, the one with flowers on the cover? Alright.*

In a way I was right. Going through the declinations was a bit like a lullaby. There is something softly harmonic in the melody of Greek. Dear Pythagoras and the music of spheres …

Just a couple of lines:

πούς, ποδός ποδί, πόδᾰ, πούς
Φωνή, φωνής, φωνή, φωνήν, φωνή.

That fear,
or more an anxiety, of not being able to read or write while having a physical job has stayed with me till today.

4.
In late April 1990, I was 9.

For the first time, and—I learned later—definitely not the last, I was sent to a psychologist due to my troubles with reading and writing. Teachers suspected dyslexia. One of the tasks among really boring tests was to draw a home.

- *Where is home?* asked the psychologist looking at my drawing of a forest.
- *At the end of the forest path …*

The note from the psychologists read: Auditory Processing Disorder, Visual Processing Disorder, Dyslexia, Crossed Laterality …

5.
In late April 1996, I was 15.

My class size was medium-large with about 28 pupils—I would say normal at that time. I don't remember the subject lesson, but we were talking about different countries and the teacher said: "Please raise hands who has never been abroad." I did. My hand was the only one.

My parents never went for holidays, not even to the close places. Maybe there were a few exceptions, which I know only through old photographs where I stare at the viewer with my bright blue eyes and albino blonde hair sitting in a pushchair. Money was one of the main reasons, but not the only one.

Abroad.
The West.
To go abroad was a myth.
The West was mystical, better, promising.
It was a myth of the West in which the West wanted to
believe. It was a myth through which the West imagined
the East.
It was a myth orientalizing
the East. It was a myth
orientalizing the West.
Everything was just the
imagination. Where was
the reality?

In the body.
It was written in, inscribed, and memorized in the body.
If you live in a society of fear, suspicion, and no trust the default of your body is to
shrink and hide. If you are a woman you have to hide even more.

As a girl, I understood the difference straight away.
I wanted to carry my body with dignity and ease, and I wanted colors.

There is this fragment in *1984* saying that the matter of choice was the matter of the aesthetics.

Yes, as well.

The West.
People often take one thing very wrong.
The fact that I wanted colors coming from an underprivileged geographical area and background did not make me feel bad. I did not perceive myself nor feel I was the worst. I never felt like a victim. I never was a victim.

It was a Western assumption put on me. It was the
West who looked at me and felt better.

It was the West which imagined itself as paradise.
And be a thankful girl if you were given a chance to be part of it!

Oh, you are from Eastern Europe, you speak English very well. It is so great that you have this job here!

They honestly thought that being a waitress is great? They honestly thought that that was my dream?

It was their image of my dream expressed in a polite way. Polite. Not always though.
Polite as long you fill the gap in the job market for the positions nobody wants to
take. Try to do something else.
Ohhh dear, you are so skilled, but that is for the native speakers, you know.
I didn't.

6.
In one of the talks, the interviewer said to Zadie Smith something like *Oh, and there you wrote this the most beautiful sentence in the English language.*

I thought I will never write the most beautiful sentence in the English language. My language will be always broken, I will write at best in International Disco Latin.
(Thank you, Hito Steyerl.)

I stopped writing.

Or perhaps Claudia Rankine was right.
I forget things too. It makes me sad. Or it makes me the saddest.
Or, perhaps, Emily Dickinson, my love, hope was never a thing with feathers.

7.
UK CITIZENS/EU   OTHER

What is your name?
What is the aim of your
visit? Where are you

going to stay? Can you
give the exact address?
Who are the people with whom you are going to stay?
Do you have money?
How much?
Can you show it?

It was asked in a formal and politically
correct way. But, it was asked. It had to be
asked. Just because of my blue passport.

I don't have to hear straight away that I am *less valued, less trusted, worth less.*
I don't have to hear *Go back from where you are from.*
It is enough that I
feel it. The
contempt might be
polite. Even very
polite.
Humiliation can be polite.

It will be written in the body.
It will be written in the memory.
And if you forget, you will
be reminded. The border.
It is enough that you understand that there are
borders. I went through this exactly eight and a
half times.
Enough as Bourdieu would say: *to understand your place.*
Or to be more precise: *the place where they see me.*

And yet, I know it is nothing in comparison to many other examples when people actually use their position of power.

8.
On May 1, 2004, Poland joined the EU, and just three days later I was waiting for my flight back to the United Kingdom. At the back of my head, I was thinking about whether I would still have to go through the same familiar border procedure. Even if the politics changed overnight, my passport did not change its color. It was still deep blue. Not the EU-burgundy. The gate next to mine had just started the boarding to one of the Scandinavian cities—I

don't remember whether it was Oslo, Copenhagen, maybe Stockholm. It looked like they were missing two passengers and quite a few times it was heard in the air: "Passengers Å and Ø please go to the gate immediately." It seemed that the passengers Å and Ø had other things to do. After a while, in the corner of my eye, like in a slow-motion scene, I saw a smiling couple holding each other's hands *running* toward the gate. It wasn't a typical fast run, more of a *La-Nouvelle-Vague*-style-run, or a run one makes in the drizzling rain in a hot summer day when it is actually blissful to feel the water on your body. They got to the closed gate laughing and—like in a movie shot—they pointed at the plane which was just disappearing in the clouds. I heard them exclaiming in this unbearably light manner: *Let's just take another one!*

I stayed in the United Kingdom just until the moment I could get back smoothly to the next academic year. When I was leaving, I hoped I would never have to get back to a physical job again. I said to my friend, half seriously, half in jest: If I come back here, it will be as a lecturer and writer. The second part was right.

9.
In late April 2007 I was 27.

It was my first year as a PhD candidate. I was studying, teaching at the university, and—in order to do all that—was working full time in a corporate office for a French outsourcing company, since my research was not funded, and I was not paid for my teaching work. My job was to pick up phone calls with a smile in my voice, saying: *Bonjour, C'est Sophie du SVP. Comment est-ce que je peux vous aider?* And then I would help people solve their IT troubles. I think it was the most boring and mindless job I've ever had, honestly. I did it in a semi-automatic way. Most of the peoples working there—except one French guy Mat—were graduates of French philology—not a dream option for ambitious graduates analyzing Sartre, Proust, or Baudelaire.

French clients knew that the help desk was not in France. I remember once that Mat, who was always nice and patient, suddenly put his conversation on the loudspeaker. I heard a pretentious scream: *You don't understand what I'm saying, I want somebody who can speak French!* And Mat, in a completely calm way, replied: *Dear sir, you are speaking to the French person.*

10.
The summer of 2018 I spent in Oslo.
It was unusually hot for this northern city.
Tre jenter satt en sommerdag på bussen i Oslo vest og snakket om den nye
kjæresten til en felles venninne.
Han er så søt.
Men begeistringen fikk en demper da den ene sjokkert kunne fortelle at han jobbet som polakk! Gutten tjente penger ved å male hus der borte på Oslo vest[2]

I hear you. Language has power. How can I say that I'm writing?

11.
In October 2019 Olga Tokarczuk won a Nobel prize for literature.
I felt happy, but perhaps more relieved.
It may sound naïve, but as a writer, I really felt relieved.
(*The voice of an immigrant is always weaker than the voice of a citizen.*)

12.
                                                          Oslo, July 2019
Dear Didier Eribon,

I'm writing to you from Oslo, where I was hoping to find a more equal society and a stable life. But especially for the latter, it has been and still is quite tough; freelance projects like writing for Norwegian or American art magazines do not pay the bills.

I'm still living in two different realities: on one hand, I curate exhibitions, give lectures, write articles, but on the other hand my current dilemma is that I worry I might meet my former students if I take up a manual labor job again for the summer.

Life seems to be written in a cruel neoliberal time schedule, constantly reminding me that for most of things, it is already too late.

I feel alienated by many things: by language, class, gender, money.
I feel alienated by the experience of an immigrant who is constantly orientalized and essentialized.
I feel cheated by the neoliberal promise that makes you believe that all you have to do is to work hard, and if you do you will get somewhere (and at the same time is so silent about all of the privileges). And for the most part I feel exhausted.
If by any miracle I stay in Oslo, and you would happen to be here, please let me know. I really hope that there are individual miracles.

13.
It is October 2019. I look at my long list of various published texts and I try not to count the rejected or thrown away. And there is hidden pile of poetry. But does it make me a writer?

14.
It is summer 2020 and I'm still in Oslo.
Perhaps it wasn't particularly economically rational, but I subscribed to *The New York Review of Books*. Whenever I take a new issue out of the mailbox, the corners of my mouth move upward.

The other day a newsletter with a poem of the day from the Poetry Foundation reached me
with the title, "For Sofia: Peniaphobia"

Sounds like fear of pennies.
From Greek: penia, poverty. Anxiety, dread,
shortness of breath, irregular heartbeat.

In the middle of a global pandemic,
with a virus causing respiratory troubles,
with protests united under the slogan "I can't breathe,"
when everything seems to be moving towards collapse
I crave for language touching reality;
I crave for our shared ability to make sense of the world.

15.
In October 2022, the House of Literature in Oslo organized lectures around Édouard Louis writings. Didier Eribon was also there. I passed him in the foyer. He never responded to my email. Was it because people who say they are proud to be

working class are really saying they are proud to no longer be working class (as he accurately remarked himself)? I don't know. The lecture "A Manifesto for the Working Class" by Édouard Louis was great and many people seemed touched. Are they the same people I meet while having my physical job who express so much contempt toward me? I don't know that either.

16.
The plane has already gone anyway.
There is something on the horizon, but is it magical?

Notes

1. The last page of the *Sun* with topless models was introduced in 1970 and survived until 2015. That's what the clients were often looking at while waiting for the food, and then often didn't bother to move the paper when the food finally arrived. So, the plate often landed on a naked girl.
2. "Three girls sat on a bus in Oslo West one summer day and talked about the new boyfriend of a mutual friend. He was so sweet. But the enthusiasm was dampened when one could tell that (shockingly) he was working as a Pole! He made money by painting houses in Oslo West." The word "polakk" ("Polish" in Norwegian) is used as a descriptive (and pejorative) term for physical work/workers since many of the Polish immigrants work as builders, carpenters, construction workers, or cleaners. Oslo West is considered a rich part of town.

TRAVIS MONTEZ

FIGURE 33.1: Travis Montez. Image by Loredo Montoneri.

THE PANIC ATTACKS returned just before Labor Day, 2016, much worse than before.

Nearly three years had passed since the last one, I'd started to believe the sudden trembles, sweating until my clothes were soaked through, and thundering chest pains were behind me.

But there I was, walking to the R train on my way to work one late August morning when I heard the window of a store being renovated shatter. Random, unexpected noises like that are a part of everyday life in Brooklyn. Normally, I doubt something like a window breaking would have gotten my attention over the music thumping from my earbuds.

This time my mind went blank and I shut my eyes closed so tightly it stung. I'd forgotten how to breathe. The muscles in my chest clenched uncontrollably, as did my fists. I needed to run or hide. Escape.

I made my way to a bench on the corner and struggled to remember the coping technique for when my anxiety spiked. After a few shallow breaths, it came back to me.

Five things you can see: eyeglass store, traffic lights, bank, man asking for money, pizzeria.

Four things you can feel: scarf, bench, coat, wallet.

Three things you can hear: walk sign buzzing, jackhammer, cars

Two things you can smell: cologne, bagels

One thing you can taste: mouthwash

I don't know how many times I repeated that. Or how long I was on that bench. But, by the time the panic receded, my suit was drenched, and I could feel tears drying on my face.

In retrospect, the return of these episodes wasn't a complete surprise.

My parents were splitting up. Again. Their marriage had been a toxic and abusive one. Their divorce, commenced a couple of months prior, and was just as full of spite. I was collateral damage of their relationship. Again. I couldn't admit it at the time, but the split—particularly my dad lashing out at his kids and trying to pit us against each other—kicked up a lot of my childhood I'd forgotten.

I hadn't been to therapy in about ten months because I convinced myself I was well and no longer needed it. I wasn't working out regularly or doing anything really to manage the obvious stress of working as a lawyer in Brooklyn Family Court.

I'd grown distant from my friends.

Laundry piled up. Dishes lived in the sink and went unwashed until they were unsalvageable and I had to throw them away.

I was barely functioning, skating the surface of a depression for the better part of a year, anxious and exhausted from pretending like I wasn't.

And I was not writing. I wasn't journaling. I wasn't jotting down ideas for my novel. I wasn't scribbling a lyric on a napkin or envelope before I lost it. I wasn't texting myself seeds that would become poems.

I hadn't been doing any of those things consistently for months.

I certainly had lots to write about. Countless unvoiced emotions coiled around each other in my mind, randomly pulsing and choking. Trapped: no particular one able to surface long enough to write about.

No writing. Not a single word.

I was depressed and in denial about my depression.

Returning to that state after "doing well" for so long seemed like a defeat to me. I had failed. I didn't want to think about it, or be honest about it. So, I couldn't or wouldn't write (about it).

Plus, part of my depressive thinking was believing that I'd never write or publish again. The certainty of that belief was a comfort because another part of my depressive thinking was that I sucked at writing.

Sure, I had good ideas, I thought, but lacked the skill to really get those ideas from my fucked-up mind out into the world in any compelling way that people gave a shit about. The fact that I'd been published, had released several collections of poetry, and performed that poetry all around the world couldn't wedge me from underneath the crush of these thoughts.

So, there was no writing, for months. My depression almost always brought anxiety to the party. So, again, it wasn't a complete surprise that right before Labor Day 2016, the sound of shattering glass made me forget how to breathe.

The panic attacks happened almost daily. Some episodes were more severe than others, but all of them were worse than what I had experienced when my anxiety disorder was diagnosed in college.

I went back into mental health treatment the following week. Therapy slowly helped me get back out into the world and into my life, a little bit at a time.

I started wanting to do things again.

After nearly a year of backing out of almost all social engagements, I forced myself to go to a play written by a friend and poetry mentor, True Rodriguez. *In Defense of Glitter and Rainbows* had its first run in a tiny theater in midtown. I caught the show's last performance in October 2016.

I went mostly to support a friend. But I think what actually got me out of the house for the first time in ages was the chance to support the kind of artist True is. Her work resonates with me because of the honest and loving manner in which she confronts themes around trauma and family. It's so inclusive and raw, but also compassionate. She manages sensitive issues with a great deal of emotional heft without being melodramatic or compromising excellence.

Her work is damn near perfect because she allows the humans represented in her art to be flawed. I admire that. I need that. And, for me, a great part of our friendship has been learning about the discipline, integrity, battles with self-doubt, ego checking, and bravery that go into being the person behind art like that.

The play managed to be even better than I expected. It hit me in a way I had not anticipated. There was a character in the play, an abusive, alcoholic father, that really struck a nerve in me. It harmonized with my hurt at that time. It helped me articulate things about my childhood I'd been discussing in therapy.

On the train ride home that night, I wrote my first poem in over a year.

Writing became an essential and intentional part of my treatment after that. And I came to realize a few things about myself that may be helpful for other creatives, particularly other creatives managing mental illness:

The part of me that is an artist is the part of me that's the most honest, most complicated, and the most complete, the freest. He's the part of me that's most human.

He's also the part of me I had gotten in the habit of neglecting most.

I also realized that my art—my writing and poetry—isn't just about what I choose to share or publish. I'm also allowed to have pieces, hell, even entire projects that are just for me.

Experimenting is important to me. I need challenges. I need to wonder.

Writing isn't just an escape or a hobby. Or a craft. It's not even just a form of self-expression or a way to entertain. For me, writing is also how I come to understand the universe inside me and connect with the world around me.

I need to create to understand myself and feel like myself.

These realizations freed me up in a number of ways. Writing, for me, had become almost exclusively about the creation of a thing that would be consumed. Published. Purchased. Read. Performed. Liked or disliked. Ignored.

This drained much of the joy from the creative process for me. When I sat down to write, that empty page was this taunting judgment, this potential and likely failure before I even put down a word.

These days, it more often feels more like an adventure or an exploration. I sit down to see what's going on, and what's possible. I often sit down and write just to wonder. Which can be boring or stressful, but also surprising and fun. A great kind of challenge. Writing like this allows for risks I don't think I was capable of taking as a younger writer.

I'm in the middle of a project now, "Objects in This Rearview," that can best be described as a multimedia epic love poem told as a trilogy. The two volumes, released in 2018, encompassed two books of poetry and a spoken word album.

An actual album!

This is something I'd never allowed myself to do before: an album with my poetry and real, original, sexy R&B/soul music. Many pieces of this project began as things I wrote to navigate my way through that bout of depression and to manage the panic attacks. It's some of my most authentic work. The truth is, I couldn't have gotten to it without support.

I have completed the manuscript for the final chapter of "Objects." What I have been especially mindful of in this creative process is how it's demanding far more collaboration than my prior work. Writing is normally a solitary process—which suits my personality. It's been such a blessing to benefit from the experience and wisdom of a creative community of folks I trust and admire. They've not only supported my vision but also expanded it.

I've always been a little intimidated by my circle of artist friends. I think they're all various kinds of brilliant and have lived in fear that one day they'd discover I was an imposter, the hack of the crew. Working through that has deepened many of my friendships and has allowed me to learn how they work through their own doubts.

Everyone's creative process is different. Figuring out mine has been essential to creating authentically and consistently. As stated before, part of that has been removing the expectation of creating a masterpiece every time I write. Or even having that as a goal.

Another piece has been a begrudging acceptance that there is no substitute for discipline. I really do need to get words on a page regularly (but recognize I am always going to be better about this sometimes than others).

I love the artist and man I've become to create "Objects in This Rearview." I want and hope that my art continues to do that: require me to grow and push myself. To learn both from the universe within me and the world without.

My art is the bridge between those places. A path I can only make by walking it.